PENGUIN BOOKS

ABRAHAM LINCOLN

Thomas Keneally won the Booker Prize in 1982 with *Schindler's Ark*, which was later made into the Academy Award–winning film *Schindler's List*. He has written nine works of nonfiction, including *The Commonwealth of Thieves*, *The Great Shame*, and *American Scoundrel*, and more than two dozen works of fiction, including *The Widow and Her Hero*, *An Angel in Australia*, and *Bettany's Book*. His novels *The Chant of Jimmie Blacksmith*, *Gossip from the Forest*, and *Confederates* were all shortlisted for the Booker Prize, while *Bring Larks and Heroes* and *Three Cheers for the Paraclete* won the Miles Franklin Award. In 1983 he was awarded the Order of Australia for his services to Australian Literature.

D0971470

THOMAS KENEALLY

Abraham Lincoln

A Life

A LIPPER™ / PENGUIN BOOK

PENGUIN BOOKS

Published by the Penguin Group

Penguin Group (USA) Inc., 375 Hudson Street, New York, New York 10014, U.S.A.

Penguin Group (Canada), 90 Eglinton Avenue East, Suite 700, Toronto,
Ontario, Canada M4P 2Y3 (a division of Pearson Penguin Canada Inc.)

Penguin Books Ltd, 80 Strand, London WC2R 0RL, England

Penguin Ireland, 25 St Stephen's Green, Dublin 2, Ireland
(a division of Penguin Books Ltd)

Penguin Group (Australia), 250 Camberwell Road, Camberwell,
Victoria 3124, Australia (a division of Pearson Australia Group Pty Ltd)

Penguin Books India Pvt Ltd, 11 Community Centre,
Panchsheel Park, New Delhi – 110 017, India

Penguin Group (NZ), 67 Apollo Drive, Rosedale, North Shore 0632,
New Zealand (a division of Pearson New Zealand Ltd)

Penguin Books (South Africa) (Pty) Ltd, 24 Sturdee Avenue,
Rosebank, Johannesburg 2196, South Africa

Penguin Books Ltd, Registered Offices:
80 Strand, London WC2R 0RL, England

First published in the United States of America by Viking Penguin,
a member of Penguin Putnam Inc. 2003
Published in Penguin Books 2008

10

ISBN 0-670-03175-5 (hc.)
ISBN 978-0-14-311475-8 (pbk.)
CIP data available

Printed in the United States of America
Set in Caslon Book
Designed by Francesca Belanger

AUTHOR'S NOTE

Rather than reproducing the erratic spelling of some of the good-faith witnesses to Lincoln's life, I have occasionally taken the liberty of standardizing the more eccentric spelling of his contemporaries, so that their intent will seem what it was: more earnest than comedic. In other cases where a witness to Lincoln's life obviously and by modern standards misspells a word, I have not found it necessary to correct the matter or insert *sic* but have instead left the matter to the reader's own corrective reading. In subtler cases involving important documents, however, an acknowledgment of the misspelling is sometimes noticed by the normal notation.

1

ABRAHAM LINCOLN WAS BORN on a mattress of corn husks in a nest of bear rugs on the morning of February 12, a Sabbath, 1809. The United States was then an infant nation with another risky war against Great Britain ahead of it. The birthplace for this new child of the republic was a one-room, windowless, dirt-floored log cabin in Hardin County, near Hodgenville in Kentucky. The cabin stood on land to which his father's title was uncertain.

Abraham's mother was a tall, bony, sinewy, undemanding woman of about twenty-five, Nancy Hanks Lincoln, a bastard child, a good wrestler on a frontier where wrestling was an important sport engaged in by both men and women. As one witness said, she was "a bold, reckless, daredevil kind of a woman, stepping to the very verge of propriety." Two years before, she had given birth to a daughter, Sarah.

For the greater part of his life, and in three states, the boy would be said to come from unrespectable stock. According to Abraham Lincoln's later law partner, William H. Herndon, there was a report that Thomas Lincoln, for a consideration from one Abraham Inlow, a miller of Elizabethtown, Kentucky, assumed the paternity of the infant child of Nancy Hanks, and though the tale does not fit with the 1806 marriage date of Tom and Nancy, the story was just one that would later haunt and help form Abraham.

Thomas was a stocky, thirty-year-old hardscrabble farmer and carpenter who had a reputation among his neighbors as a raconteur, a fact that gives some support to the idea that he was the boy's biological father, for Abraham would all his life sprout with rustic tales and parables to an extent that sometimes bemused even his friends. Thomas meant to call the child Abraham after his father, a pioneer from Virginia, whom in 1786—when Thomas was a little boy—he had seen killed before his eyes by British-allied Indians.

Plagued by Kentucky's uncertain land titles, Tom Lincoln moved his family, when Abraham was still an infant, ten miles to a 230-acre farm on Knob Creek. Of sturdy Tom Lincoln many contradictory things are said—that he was industrious, that he was lazy; that he was shiftless, that he had the pioneer spirit; that he was proud of the intellectual leanings of his frontier son, and that he punished Abraham for them. One thing is certain—that Tom was in his way an archetype of the Protestant subsistence farmer, who, according to Thomas Jefferson's dream, was the stuff of American virtue and the fit occupier of the frontier. Tom and his type would inherit the American earth without recourse to the corrupting influence of banks, and though they might not be able to read and write with any fluency, their native wisdom and their democratic impulse would derive directly from the ennobling soil. Tom Lincoln was probably unaware in any explicit way that he embodied that ideal, but the boy early on refused to buy the concept. Where Jefferson believed he saw forthright independence, Lincoln saw ignorance and brutalizing labor. He would not grow up admiring his hardhanded father.

And though, in growing, Abraham developed a body and a physical endurance appropriate to a frontier boy, his spirit was always uneasy in the backwoods. When he was nominated a candidate for his presidency and was being harried by a Chicago newspaperman, John L. Scripps, for information on his childhood for a campaign biography, Abraham quoted Gray's *Elegy:* "'The short and simple annals of the poor.' That's my life, and that's all you or anyone else can make of it."

In Knob Creek, at six years of age, Abraham began to learn his letters from a slave-owning Catholic teacher in a log schoolhouse on the Cumberland Road. This institution was what they called on the frontier a "blab school," where students learned by rote. There, with his older sister, Sarah, during one brief session in 1815 and another the following year, Abraham learned to write his name and to count.

His parents worshiped at an antislavery Baptist church. That controversial allegiance in a slave state and constant title fights over the Knob Creek farm made Thomas decide that they would be better off in the newly proclaimed, more exactly surveyed Indiana Territory. Thus the family became early Hoosiers, a name originally applied to Indiana settlers arriving from the South. Tom Lincoln went off first, with his possessions on a flatboat, down Salt Creek and into the Ohio, then ashore to reconnoiter for a farm. He found a location sixteen miles in from the river, near the small town of Gentryville. The family, when they moved, did so on foot, accompanying the bullock wagon carrying their goods. Rather late in the year, they came to Tom's claim of 160 acres of dense thickets, in the Little Pigeon Creek community. Here Tom and Nancy again sought membership in an antislavery Baptist church. For their first three months there, eight-year-old Abraham and his family lived in the three-sided "pole-shed" that Tom had constructed hurriedly to deal with the imperatives of the season. The open side of the shed faced south, away from the prevailing wind and snow, and a large fire was kept going there day and night. Here, with either snow or the smoke of that fire billowing in the hut, Abraham and Sarah ingested Bible tales as narrated by Nancy, and the founding principles of their Calvinist view of the world, together with sundry peasant superstitions about phases of the moon, ghosts, and other matters. The young Lincoln, socially precocious enough to call out to passersby and thus to earn his father's anger, was already a farm laborer and experienced the demanding but bodybuilding life of a farm boy—helping his father clear fields, split rails, plow, and thresh wheat. But as for the complete stereotype of the backwoods boy: Once, seeing a wild turkey approach the farm, Abraham fetched a gun and shot it from within his own doorway. The experience of destroying animal life, of seeing the gush of blood, repelled him, and he would never become the deadeye frontier marksman of American myth.

Nancy Lincoln's aunt and uncle, the Sparrows, arrived in Indiana on the Lincolns' heels, carrying in tow the semiliterate bastard child of one of Nancy's sisters, one Dennis Hanks. Between the boy Lincoln and the adolescent Dennis, a lout in the eyes of some, an intense friendship developed. Those who disapproved of Abraham Lincoln's later tendency to tell off-color stories often attributed the habit to Dennis's influence. But

Dennis did not like the way Tom Lincoln treated the boy, and would influence Lincoln's earliest biographers to judge Tom rather severely.

The boy Lincoln had had many mysterious experiences of the will of that Calvinist God to whom most of America was in thrall. He had already lost a baby brother, Tom. And now, in the summer of 1818, a visitation of the disease the settlers called "the milk sick" struck the Little Pigeon Creek area. Manifesting itself in the white-coated tongues of the sufferers, it was believed to be passed through the milk of cows that had eaten of the poisonous white snakeroot, and were themselves doomed. The Sparrows caught the disease first and died while being nursed by Nancy, whom Dennis Hanks would later honor as the most affectionate woman he had ever met. Falling ill herself, Nancy died with seven days, unattended by a doctor—since there was none—and calling Sarah and Abraham to her bedside. Tom Lincoln fashioned her coffin from black cherrywood, and she lay in state in the one-room cabin before making her final mile-long journey to a grave on a knoll in the woods. She was thirty-four years old, but already withered and toothless, like many a frontier woman.

Tom Lincoln took Dennis Hanks in, and he slept with Abraham in the loft. For the entirety of the bitter winter, twelve-year-old Sarah became the woman of the household, with all the chores involved in that description. Then, in the spring, after planting, Tom Lincoln left the farm in the care of Dennis, Abraham, and Sarah and headed down to Kentucky to propose marriage to a woman he had admired from boyhood, the recently widowed Sarah "Sally" Johnston. Sally was healthy and of a positive mentality and a more elevated class than Nancy.

She had some furniture, including a fine bureau; and after the marriage Tom loaded it all up on his wagon and took it over the Ohio, along with his new bride and her three children, who would become Abraham and Sarah's stepbrother and -sisters. Not only did Abe now make a close acquaintance with his first feather mattress, pillows ditto, with a bureau and proper kitchen chairs instead of stools, but the tall Sally proved another kindly mother. Lincoln would later say that she was his best friend in the world. She saw that Abraham and Dennis Hanks were dressed mainly in buckskins, and introduced them to a better kind of denim clothing. She also insisted that Tom Lincoln lay down a floor in the cabin, and put in some windows.

Dennis Hanks liked Sally too, but again said of Thomas that he treated his precocious boy "rather unkindly than otherwise, always appeared to think much more of his stepson John D. Johnston than he did of his own son Abraham."

Despite the rawness of the Lincolns, their lives now did take on some signs of the Arcadian settler life envisioned by Jefferson. The government was selling land at $1.25 an acre, and Thomas bought one hundred acres. His carpentry was so much in demand that he was given the largely volunteer job of building the Little Pigeon Creek Baptist Church. The young Abraham, pressed into work as sexton, probably heard many of the minister's antislavery sermons, and they may have reinforced his inchoate sense that slavery was the founding serpent in the American garden.

Tom Lincoln hired his son out to other farmers at twenty-five cents a day, especially after the age of eleven, when he began to shoot up in height and demonstrated a particular gift with the ax. Occasionally he attended the school of one Hazel

Dorsey, a mile and a half from the Lincoln farm. He brought to that log school a chaotic hunger for literacy, fostered by his stepmother, Sally, who nearly fifty years later would say, in remembrance that had a ring of authenticity to it, "I induced my husband to permit Abe to read and study at home as well as at school. At first he was not easily reconciled to it."

Physically Abraham resembled his late mother. As he reached puberty, he developed a capacity for the spellbinding telling of proper and—in notable number—improper stories. Somewhere he acquired a collection of indecent jokes named *Quin's Jests,* which he read at night to a delighted, barely literate Dennis. Abraham remembered its contents as he did everything he read.

His occasional schooling was fitted in between winter harvest and spring planting. Apart from Webster's and Dillworth's *Spelling Books,* both of which had improving tales in them, one cornerstone of Abraham's adolescent reading would be Parson Weems's *Life of Washington;* and another, Defoe's *Robinson Crusoe. Aesop's Fables,* Bunyan's *Pilgrim's Progress,* the Bible—all these had a formative influence on the strange mixture of the sonorous and the rustic that would characterize his discourse. A family copy of *Barclay's Dictionary* enlarged his armory of words.

The marks of the adolescent Lincoln were his buckskin clothing (and the fact that he was always growing comically too tall for his pants) and the ridicule this attracted from girls, so that he would never be fully comfortable with women; his capacity for reading, and the fact that by frontier standards he was precociously literate; and—once again—his strength. "[Y]ou would say there was three men at work by the way the trees fell," said one acquaintance of Abraham's axmanship.

Contradictorily, though, Dennis Hanks argued that, "Lincoln was lazy. . . . He was always reading—scribbling—writing—ciphering—even Sally Lincoln would admit that he wouldn't like physical labor, though he had the strength for it, but was 'diligent for Knowledge.'" He was also making things difficult for his future promoters by developing skepticism about predestination, about the God of Calvinism, who had from eternity damned many and saved a few. What sort of God was it who would create human beings, having known from eternity that he would damn some of them and save others? In the words of Abraham's favorite poet, Burns, a God who:

> Sends ane to heaven and ten to hell
> A' for thy glory,
> And no one for ony guid or ill
> They've done afore thee!

It was a conundrum that concerned many sensitive souls in nineteenth-century America, and despite his rugged body, Abraham was such a soul. His sister, Sarah, had married one Aaron Grigsby, whom Abraham Lincoln did not like. When Abraham was seventeen years of age, she and the child to whom she was trying to give birth both perished. Here was God's inscrutable will at work once more, its irrationality a further test to young Lincoln's soul, which both despised yet yearned for the comforts of ordinary belief.

Abraham had taken to hiring himself out for books now, rather than store goods. Thus he acquired Caleb Bingham's *The American Preceptor* and *Columbian Orator,* both designed to equip youth for the arts of eloquence. Similarly he showed an enthusiasm for rivers, as a way out of puzzles. Little Pigeon Creek might have been "the most unpoetical place on earth," and forest-locked, but the currents of the western river system promised arrival at places designed for reinvention of the self. At the confluence of the Anderson and Ohio Rivers he worked at ferrying travelers to meet steamers or to go south into Kentucky. One day he rowed two businessmen out into midstream in his cockboat to catch an oncoming steamer. As they climbed aboard, both men threw a silver half-dollar into the bottom of Lincoln's boat.

It is hard for us to imagine how momentous an event this was for an Indiana farm boy. Despite the modest accumulation of specie Tom had put together for buying acreage, the Lincolns had never lived on a regular basis in the cash economy. Tom Lincoln did not pay for things: He grew his own wheat, corn, and vegetables; tanned his own leather; made clothing out of buckskin, cotton, and flax of his own raising; and when he bought sugar and coffee from the store in nearby Gentryville, paid for them with hogs, venison hams, and coonskins. Abraham's labor was generally paid for in store goods. But now he saw, glinting on the boards of his boat, his liberation from the cashless world in which brain-numbing labor and raw muscle were respected over scholarship. Here too was the true fuel of those improvements in roads, canals, and river navigation that would be the chief element of his burgeoning political ideas.

Later, in the White House, he would say of this incident, "Gentlemen, you may think it a very little thing . . . but it was the most important incident of my life . . . the world seemed wider and fairer before me."

2

WHEN SPRING CAME in 1828, James Gentry, the storekeeper who gave his name to Gentryville, planned to send a flatboat loaded with grain, meat, sugar, and tobacco down to New Orleans. Gentry's son Allen, a friend of Abraham's, was the captain of the vessel, and Lincoln himself signed on as the bow hand. They departed from Rockport on the Ohio, the river that served as the Indiana-Kentucky border. They poled their way down the Ohio and into the Mississippi, whose current carried them into the different world of Spanish moss and institutional slavery. While they were tied up at a plantation near Baton Rouge, where they were trading some of their cargo, their raft was attacked at night by a group of seven slaves armed with knives. Abe and the Gentry boy, roused from their sleep, grabbed clubs and in the end drove the men off. Many would speculate later on what would have befallen America if the ultimate Great Emancipator had been killed on the Mississippi in 1828 by those he would later free.

New Orleans was the biggest town Abraham had ever seen, where seven thousand flatboats like the one he traveled on sat ready to sell their cargoes, and where the architectural elegance of the French Quarter and the squalor of the slave pens stated the contradictory nature of the South. Since their flatboat, once they had sold its cargo, was disposable, on part of their trip home they caught a steamer. Arriving back, Abraham had twenty-five dollars' cash money to give his father.

Thus, that summer young Lincoln had acquired some leisure to hang around the courts in Rockport and Boonville and to acquire a copy of the popular *Revised Statutes of Indiana*. For the first time he read the Declaration of Independence and the Constitution, for he noticed how frequently lawyers in court called upon them.

There was a great deal of information in Indiana about new land opportunities in Illinois, beyond the Wabash River. Dennis Hanks, who had married one of Abe's stepsisters, lost a lot of stock in the winter of 1829 to the milk sick, and so did Thomas Lincoln. He sold his land to James Gentry, and his grain and stock to another Indiana settler, and in early 1830 headed west in a wagon drawn by two yokes of oxen. Illinois had already voted to be a nonslave state, but it would be wrong to believe that in moving to southern Illinois, Tom was making a statement of fraternity with the enslaved black man. Like most newcomers to Illinois, he saw the black man both as the property of Southern aristocrats, whom he resented, and as a potential source of competition for labor, keeping down wages—such as they were—in kind or cash. Whatever the comprehensive motives for this shift, one of them was, perhaps, that a Hanks relative was already settled in Macon County, Illinois, and had sent promising reports.

The large party of Lincolns, thirteen in all, including Dennis and his wife, made their way over the swollen streams and unthawed tracks into Illinois. Their wagon was nearly swept away in crossing the swollen Kaskaskia. They settled to the west of

Decatur, "on the North Side of the Sangamon River, at the junction of the timber-land and prairie."

Here Abe, just turned twenty-one, helped his father cut the timbers for and build another cabin, clear ten acres, and plant corn. By this time, father and son, working together, were strangers. Books like Abe's copy of *The Revised Statutes of Indiana* had increased the distance between them.

Abraham began to go to political meetings in the summer. At one meeting outside a store in Decatur—when he heard a local politician speak unimpressively on the issue of dredging the Sangamon, so that local traders could avail themselves of a current to take them down to New Orleans—Lincoln made his first passionate speech on the issue. As one who heard him said later, in its advocacy for public works, for what we now call infrastructure, it was typical of speeches he would make for the next twenty years.

That autumn everybody in the Lincoln family came down with what they called "the ague"—a form of malarial fever. Surviving, they then faced a memorable winter—the "winter of the deep snow," as it would be called—in which cattle and horses wallowed in powder and died of exhaustion. After his brief display of rhetoric in Decatur, rural fever and snow had put Lincoln back in his place.

But the Sangamon flowed into the Mississippi via the Illinois and thus offered Abraham yet another potential road. With his stepbrother, John Johnston, and John Hanks, a cousin on his mother's side, Abraham was planning to take another flatboat of cargo to New Orleans. A speculator-storekeeper named Denton Offut would supply the cargo. The young men set to work on the flatboat on the banks of the Sangamon. Eighteen feet wide and eighty feet long, according to John Hanks, it was loaded with barrel pork and corn, and would pick up live hogs farther downriver. Just abreast of the village of New Salem, this huge, laden raft got stuck on the milldam wall. Onlooking locals were impressed to see the way the tallest boatman took control, ordering the unloading of a large part of the cargo and then boring a hole in the bow to let just enough water through to tip the whole great raft forward and over the weir. Offut was also very taken with this exploit of Abe's, and formed the intention to offer this competent young man a job.

The flatboat rushed through Beardstown, pushed along by a sail constructed of planks. ("The people came out and laughed at them," said one contemporary.) They entered the Mississippi where it made a great bend above St. Louis. Where the Ohio joined the Mississippi, they passed Cairo, a southern Illinois river port that would have prodigious importance in an as yet unenvisaged war, and they stopped at Memphis, Vicksburg, and Natchez to trade. John Hanks remembered the impact of revisiting New Orleans on Abraham. "There it was when we saw Negroes chained, maltreated, whipped, and scourged. Lincoln saw it; his heart bled, said nothing much. . . . I can say, knowing it, that it was on this trip that he formed his opinions of slavery. It ran its irons in him then and there, May 1831."

Offut, having traveled south more comfortably on a river steamer, met Abe, John Hanks, and the Johnston boy in New Orleans to oversee the sale of his cargo, and then returned with them to St. Louis by steamer, from which he veered off to attend some business. The three flatboatmen walked from there into the interior of Illinois, a hike of a mere hundred miles or so.

• • •

In Abe's absence Tom Lincoln had moved his family to his last farm in Coles County. But Denton Offut, while in New Salem, had purchased the mill and decided to open a general store, and asked Abe to clerk for him. New Salem was a small place on the bluffs above the river, but it was a definite and discrete town, with its politics, its gangs, its street life. So the twenty-two-year-old took the job and left his father's influence more or less for good.

When Lincoln first arrived in town in his rough homespun pants that were several inches too short, one townsperson considered him "as ruff a specimen of humanity as could be found." Another remembered, "His appearance was very odd." The local doctor, Dr. Jason Duncan, "found something about the young man very attractive, evincing intelligence, far beyond the generality of youth. . . ." People remembered that in Offut's store Lincoln read purposefully between customers, even for just five minutes at a time. One later friend's first sighting was in a local house, Lincoln lying on a trundle bed rocking a cradle with his foot while reading. Another villager remembered him atop a wood heap, reading a statute book. He also had a book in hand as he walked from group to group along the street.

He was popular because of his whimsical sense of humor. Despite his poor clothing, his blue jeans, "a coarse pare of Stoga shoes," and a "low crowned broad-brimmed hat," he was a good and obliging clerk. He swapped jokes with farmers in the store, and competed in sprints and wood-chopping events. He went fishing with a dropout schoolteacher named Jack Kelso, a passionate admirer of Shakespeare, and, by fishing holes along the riverbank, argued the merits of the Bard's plays and soliloquies. He joined a local debating society that met in an old storehouse, and dared express there some of the skepticism about the Bible that he had picked up from reading Tom Paine. He told one friend that the history of the New Testament showed Christ to be a bastard, and his mother a base woman. Lincoln did not belong to any church but seemed to subscribe to the tradition of deism, the concept of something like a grand overriding cosmic intelligence, a divine architect. He still fought with the concept of predestination, the tenet of the preaching houses of the hinterland.

Early in his stay in New Salem he became the butt of a group called the Clary Grove Boys and their leader, Jack Armstrong. These were the hardfisted mockers of all oddity in the place. But though Abraham may have been odd, he was big. A wrestling match was organized, with Offut and Bill Clary, another storekeeper, acting as promoters. Bets were made; a date was chosen. It seems that Jack Armstrong applied an illegal hold to Lincoln, who stood back and reproached him. Lincoln's enormous strength became apparent to everyone when he put Armstrong on his back. According to a number of versions, the Clary Grove Boys did not seem to like this, but Armstrong called them off a defiant Lincoln and became his friend and admirer for life.

The wrestling match gave Abraham great social credit in New Salem. But then, so did one of his jokes about a preacher who got a possum caught in his pants. Encouraged by reading Tom Paine, the poetry of Robbie Burns, and Constantine Volney's religion-deflating *Ruins,* he wrote in 1834 his own "Little Book on Infidelity" attacking the divinity of Christ, the veracity of the Bible, and the logicality of predestination. He wanted to send it to newspapers for publication. A storekeeper's wife, a friend of Lincoln's, Parthena Hill, remembered her wise husband, Sam, snatching it from its author's hands and burning it in the fire. It was a great favor, for the tract would have had the capacity to destroy the young man politically.

At the age of twenty-three, in early 1832, he announced himself a candidate for the state legislature. His political platform, his first published piece of writing, was printed in the March 15, 1832, issue of Springfield's *Sangamo Journal*. He declared himself a supporter of "improvements." This was a more heretical idea to some than it would seem now. Improvements required the existence of financing banks, and Democrats abominated banks as an Old World perversion from which the Jeffersonian farmer should be saved. Lincoln's political prophet, Henry Clay of Kentucky, had devised a model he named the "American System": subsidies for internal improvements (such as widening the Sangamon, a beloved project of the young Abraham, the digging of canals, and the laying of railroads) and a national bank to create a uniform system of national investment and currency. The party Clay had turned into a modern machine went by the name Whigs, a title borrowed from the British liberal progressives, and Abraham was a Whig, standing for a different world from the one Tom Lincoln occupied.

After laying out the Clay vision in his platform as published in the local paper, the young Abraham said eloquently, "I was born and have ever remained in the most humble walks of life. I have no wealthy or popular relatives or friends to recommend me. My case is thrown exclusively upon the independent voters of the county. . . ." It was not yet remarkable prose in itself, but it was remarkable prose for Tom Lincoln's son, and a long way from the adolescent exercises of his copybook:

Abraham Lincoln is my nam[e]
And with my pen I wrote the same
I wrote in both hast and speed
and left it here for fools to read

As for his oratory, a campaign speech ran, "My politics is short and sweet, like an old woman's dance. I am in favor of a national bank, a high and protective tariff, and the internal improvement system. If elected, I will be thankful. If beaten, I can do as I have been doing, work for a living." Here at the start is Lincoln's western pithiness and lack of pretense. He spoke in an idiom to which the novels of Mark Twain would give an international currency.

Offut's store was failing for want of river traffic, and so a riverboat, the *Talisman,* was attracted up from the Illinois to save the place from its own shallows. Offut persuaded Captain Bogue Vincent to use Abraham Lincoln as his Sangamon River pilot, for Lincoln knew all its shoals. If the *Talisman* could become a regular visitor, it would restore river commerce to New Salem and give fresh value to the land Offut owned there. But not even Abraham, standing in the bow and cutting overhanging branches as the steamer progressed, could get the *Talisman* to New Salem. As the craft abandoned the attempt and steamed off again to St. Louis, Offut's store crashed and Lincoln became unemployed.

Lincoln's political campaign had just begun, and his employment by Offut had come to an end, when a military diversion was thrust on him. An elderly leader of the Fox and the Sauk Indians, Black Hawk, had as a young man been driven with his people into Iowa, as a result of an unsatisfactory treaty with the United States in 1804. The Fox and the Sauk had sided with the British in 1812, in the hope that they might vanquish the Americans and arrest their settlement of Illinois. But when the British were defeated, these indigenous peoples were deprived even of the Iowa land they previously held and were allocated a less favorable stretch of earth. Hungry, and pressed from the north by other tribes including the Dakota, in the spring of 1842 they were led back by Black Hawk to their homeland across the Mississippi, the Rock River region of northern Illinois. Black Hawk announced with some dignity that he intended to plant corn on his traditional ground, but in trying to do so, he and his warriors violated both the earlier and the more recent treaties.

A boy raised with the tale of his grandfather's slaughter at the hands of Indian marauders in Kentucky, Lincoln never seemed to think it a national sin that Indians were forced off their land to make way for settlers—the way he did when black men and women were kept in bondage to enhance the wealth of Southern property owners. Though his enlistment in the militia for the summer might have had a certain political expedience to it, and he intended to return to New Salem in time for the election in late August, he went off to campaign on a borrowed horse because he believed devoutly that the settlers of the Rock River Valley should be free from Indian molestation. When the Coles County Company of which he was a member rendezvoused at a place called Rushville, Lincoln was elected its captain. In total, four regiments and a spy battalion formed in the country between Beardstown and Rushville, and they marched toward the mouth of Rock River.

Abraham Lincoln relished his command—later, he would say that no other success in his life had given him as much satisfaction as being elected captain. One acquaintance remembered that Lincoln "had the wildest company in the world," but he drilled them in the important maneuver of shifting from column into line. And in the process of chasing Black Hawk and his band of five hundred across northern Illinois, Lincoln made some important friends. One was a brigade major of militia named John Todd Stuart, a Springfield lawyer and a powerful figure among the Whigs of Illinois; another was Orville Hickman Browning, who would one day escort President-elect Lincoln from Springfield to his inauguration in Washington. Stuart's first impressions of Abraham were of his strength and skill in wrestling and athletic sports, and that he was "a great lover of jokes and teller of stories." The only disapproval he attracted had been early in the campaign, when his men, who included many of the Clary Grove Boys, broke into the wagon that held the officers' whiskey supply. The senior command punished Lincoln by making him bear a wooden sword for two days.

Unlike politicians who seek to make all they can of their military service, Lincoln later self-mockingly described his as involving many bloody encounters with mosquitoes and many dashing and hungry assaults on wild onion patches and stray pigs. For in the muddy, swampy pursuit up the Rock River, in company with Capt. Zachary Taylor's regulars, Lincoln's company got very low on food. Many of his men considered their duty done once Black Hawk and his warriors passed into Wisconsin. But Lincoln signed up for a further month—he had no store to go back to—and then for a further month, even when he had to serve as a private.

During his militia service he had an encounter with a prostitute in Beardstown and, according to another source, one in Galena. Herndon later said Lincoln had told him he had suffered from syphilis, and whether that was true or not, fear of passing the disease on would make Lincoln anxious about marrying.

Later in his service, he and his comrades came across five whites recently killed by Black Hawk's party. "[E]very man had a round, red spot on top of his head." They had been scalped. Such experience would no doubt influence the fierce behavior of the regulars when ultimately they caught up with Black Hawk's group in Wisconsin.

By then, his third month of soldiering over, Lincoln returned to New Salem for more electioneering. The respect of fellow soldiers and officers had given him fresh confidence. In the election he came in eighth in a field of thirteen. At the New Salem polling station itself, however, more than three-quarters of his fellow citizens gave him their vote. For that reason he wondered whether he could afford to leave New Salem, his political base. A contradictory temptation, however, was to study law, as Major Stuart had urged him, and to enter a wider world.

Among the friends Abe made with whom he renewed contact on his return to New Salem was the daughter of the Rutledges of Rutledge's Tavern, Ann. Lincoln had been at various times a boarder at the Tavern. Ann was young—nineteen when Lincoln first met her—well educated by the standards of New Salem, an appealing young woman. There was an understanding between her and a young man from back East, who suddenly confessed that he must travel to attend to his late father's business and said he would ultimately return to New Salem to marry her. Billy Herndon would later claim that Ann Rutledge was the only woman Lincoln ever really loved, and the longer Ann Rutledge's fiancé remained away from New Salem, the higher Abraham Lincoln's hopes were said to rise. Some friends would later claim that Ann was merely a friend, but legend has her as his truest love.

3

In 1832 Abraham formed a partnership with William F. Berry, a preacher's son, to buy Offut's store. Soon after, another New Salem store became available, and Lincoln and Berry took it over too—there was some talk that its owner had been driven out by the Clary Grove Boys. The entire purchase was made possible through the acceptance of promissory notes, by which Lincoln and Berry assumed a considerable debt payable to sundry genial New Salemites who believed in them. Billy Herndon asserted that no more unfortunate partner than Berry could have been found. "For while Lincoln was at one end of the store dispensing political information, Berry at the other was disposing of the firm's liquors.... Lincoln's application to Shakespeare and Burns was only equaled by Berry's attention to Spiggott and Barrel." The business struggled. By the following spring, two brothers purchased the store from Lincoln and Berry, but before their notes fell due, they in turn had gone broke and fled without paying a cent. Lincoln could have sought refuge in bankruptcy. But there was a rectitude in him, a seriousness about capital, that compelled him to assume and pay off, over the better part of the next few decades, the entire debt. Apart from the impact on his honor, a failure to do so would have destroyed his only political base, though it was an increasingly dwindling one, at New Salem.

In 1833, probably through the good offices of influential friends, the Democratic president, Andrew Jackson, was persuaded to appoint Lincoln postmaster at New Salem. The wages were thirty dollars per annum, not enough to make a dent in his financial burden, which with typical irony he named the "national debt." The post office, however, did not occupy him continuously, despite the fact that his frontier scrupulousness had him pursuing for miles a customer who had overpaid for postage, and taking time-consuming pains to hunt down the addressees of letters. The rest of the time he cut rails, worked at the mill or sawmill, and helped out with harvests and in New Salem's surviving stores.

The surveyor of Sangamon also offered to depute to Lincoln any surveying work within his part of the county, and so Abraham procured a compass and chain, studied surveying books "a little," and went at it. In this task, which took him to many parts of the county, his amiability impressed the citizenry. The people of Coles County became used to the sight of the gangling postmaster-surveyor hauling his instruments across a complicated and heavily wooded landscape, with letters stuck into his hatband for delivery to farms along the way.

Some notes he had signed to avoid bankruptcy became due for payment in 1834. Creditors sued, and the sheriff took possession of his horse, bridle, and surveying instruments. But a friend, a farmer named Jimmy Short, bought them at auction and returned them to him. Lincoln's partner died soon after— Herndon says because of the ruin alcoholism had wrought on his constitution. Since the "national debt" included Berry's share, it reached a total of eleven hundred dollars. It is a credit to people's belief in him that from then on there were few further prosecutions over the debt—most waited for Lincoln to pay it off because they believed he would, and in full. This assumption of his honesty was reflected in the voting for the legislature in 1834. He depended purely on the range of voters he had gotten to know through his service in the Black Hawk War, and through his work as postmaster and surveyor. In an era of multiple representation for each county, Lincoln came in a close second in a field of thirteen candidates, and so found himself a state assemblyman, soon to go off to represent Henry Clay's Whigs in the state capital at Vandalia. Among the other successful candidates was his lawyer friend John Todd Stuart, whom Lincoln had outpolled but who might, even at the risk of his own chances, have directed some votes that would have gone to him to the talented Abraham. Stuart believed in Lincoln as a man with political gifts, although one senior man in the party asked on first sighting Lincoln, "Can't the party raise any better material than that?"

In icy weather, with eight fellow politicians—six representatives and two senators—Lincoln caught the stagecoach to Vandalia. Assemblyman Lincoln was twenty-five years old, six feet four inches tall in his stockings, stoop-shouldered, long-legged, large-footed. One witness said that he had longer arms than any human he'd ever seen, "and letting his arms fall down his Sides, the points of his fingers would touch a point lower on his legs by nearly three inches than was usual with other persons." The same witness described how when some "mirth-inspiring Story" came to his mind, his countenance would light up, "several wrinkles would diverge from the inner corner of his eyes, and extending down and diagonally across his nose, his eyes would Sparkle, all terminating in an unrestrained Laugh in which everyone present, willing or unwilling, were compelled to take part." Yet his fellow travelers noticed that he did not stoke his powers of narration with liquor. Whiskey, he said, left him "flabby and undone." For the journey to the state capital, Lincoln wore "a very respectable looking suit of jeans," not the highest level of fashion but in accordance with the spirit of Henry Clay's party—to wear jean cloth was a statement of support for American manufacturers.

Vandalia was a town of eight hundred souls around a muddy square with an already decrepit brick statehouse. It stood in a prairie landscape through which covered wagons regularly passed. For accommodation, legislators were crammed into taverns and boardinghouses, cheek by jowl, and got to know each other very well. Here, for the first term, Lincoln shared a room across from the capitol with his mentor, Stuart. In Vandalia for the first time he sighted a newly arrived Democrat from Vermont, a heavy-drinking cock sparrow of a man, short and dumpy, Stephen A. Douglas. Lincoln and Douglas would be locked together in discourse over slavery and other matters for the better part of three decades. But Douglas, already a lawyer, would for most of that time far outstrip his rival in repute and standing.

So it became increasingly clear to the eloquent bumpkin from New Salem that to become a lawyer was to enter a doorway to power. Lincoln had been studying Blackstone's *Commentaries* and other legal texts since the Black Hawk War, and Vandalia reinforced his determination to pursue that path.

Although there were party structures in the politics of Illinois, they were not as fixed as in modern times, and Stuart later said that he was not above trading off Lincoln's vote on local matters. Stuart told the story of a case in which this happened—

a legislator who roomed across the hall from him and Lincoln was promoting a railroad to be built on the credit of the state of Illinois. "Lincoln and I made a trade with Breeze [the legislator in question] to the effect that we would help pass his railroad bill if he would help us secure the appointment of the Canal Commissioners by the Governor." Thus Stuart was able to get three Whigs—men who believed in public improvements—appointed as commissioners.

In his first session Lincoln was industrious, serving on twelve special committees and as a secretary to the leading Whigs, including Stuart. Stuart used Lincoln as a handy Whig orator on the chamber floor, and persuaded him to take on the job of being legislative correspondent for the *Sangamo Journal*, writing hundreds of unsigned anti-Democratic editorials. In the spirit of Henry Clay he supported a bill for a state-chartered bank in Springfield, and the Illinois and Michigan Canal. He introduced an internal improvements bill of his own, for a toll bridge across Salt Creek in Sangamon County, but he could not get it to its first reading.

The session earned him a welcome $258, and after returning along the freezing road to New Salem, he resumed his law studies. He still did local surveying jobs, and performed the tasks of postmaster, but there were indications that he was overworking himself.

When Lincoln returned to Vandalia in December for the next session, Stuart was running for the U.S. Congress, which left some room for Lincoln to expand in importance as a Whig leader. He was the chief spokesman for the interests of Sangamon County, for the dream that it would be connected by river and other transportation improvements to the wider world. It was interesting that he had no assets of his own to protect—his support for the "American System" was purely ideological. Never did such an impoverished man speak so well for the interests of American capital. His notable initiative was the introduction of a bill for a Beardstown and Sangamon canal company. His activism during this session would help assuage the extreme melancholy produced by the death of Ann Rutledge.

As her brother later told Billy Herndon, Ann consented in the end to renounce the absentee suitor and to take Abe's hand, with the one proviso that he give her time to write to her betrothed in the East. It was also arranged that she would give Lincoln time to build his fortune before marrying him. But in the high summer of 1835, with Abe's fortune not yet achieved, and no reply from her former suitor, she died of an unspecified fever—probably typhoid brought on by the flooding and pollution of the water supply.

After the death, said a witness, Abraham seemed quite changed, depressed and given to solitude. "But various opinions obtained as to the cause of his change, some thought it was an increased application to his *Law studies,* others that it was deep anguish of *Soul* (as he was all soul) over the Loss of Miss R."

Whether he loved her or not, he did mourn her death profoundly—the sudden obliteration of this fine young woman. A number of witnesses talk about his depression and melancholy becoming more and more apparent. He called his recurrent and severe melancholia the "hypo"; it would be his abiding companion.

But he was involved with another woman as well—Mary Owens, a Kentucky woman whom he had earlier met and corresponded with, and whose New Salem aunt had now brought her up to Sangamon County with the clear intention of clinching a betrothal. Lincoln was shocked to see how Mary had aged, and how her skin had coarsened; yet he felt honor bound to court her, since he had earlier shown enthusiasm. He did harbor at the time sincere doubts about his capacity to support a wife or indeed to be a decent husband, and so out of both self-interest and self-doubt he dithered. Mary remained a hopeful friend and soul mate.

Lincoln announced his candidacy for reelection in 1836 with another apparently casual letter in the *Sangamo Journal*. "Whether elected or not, I go for distributing the proceeds of the sales of the public lands to the several states. . . ." If he was alive on the first Monday in November, he said, he would vote for the Whig candidate for the presidency, Hugh L. White. One of Lincoln's fellow Whig candidates in this campaign was his future brother-in-law, Ninian W. Edwards, an elegant Kentuckian who knew he was socially Abraham's superior. The Whig Party was far more a party of the well-educated gentry and bourgeois townfolk than of such unfashionable frontier yokels-on-the-rise as Abe Lincoln.

The campaign was ferocious. Lincoln once drew a pistol on a Democrat opponent during a debate in Springfield, but at another meeting he stopped a brawl between Democrats and Whigs (including Edwards). In fact, a number of witnesses remarked on his ability as a pacifier. He spoke, said one witness, in a "tenor intonation of voice that ultimately settled down into that clear, shrill, monotone Style of Speaking, that enabled his audience, however large, to hear distinctly the lowest Sound in his voice."

When Lincoln went to Vandalia this time, he was a prominent member of the Long Nine, nine lanky and mainly young legislators from the Sangamon area. Abe was the longest of the Long Nine, and Stuart's departure left him "the acknowledged leader of the Whigs in the House. Stuart had gone out and left him a clear field." The Long Nine had resolved among themselves to trade their votes in such a way as to ensure that the state capital should be moved to Springfield, the chief city of Sangamon County. Abe also supported what would prove in time to be a disastrous series of measures for the building of roads, canals, and railroads in Illinois, to be financed by state bonds to the value of ten million dollars. A man who was still struggling to repay a debt of eleven hundred dollars nonetheless supported with passion what was, for its day, a massive scheme.

Even as a notable speaker on the floor, Abe still carried the marks of his origins. "He made a good many speeches in the Legislature," noted one witness, "mostly on local subjects. A close observer, however, could not fail to see that the tall six footer, with his homely logic, clothed in the language of the humbler classes, had the stuff in him to make a man of mark."

Significantly Lincoln and another Sangamon County colleague, Dan Stone, had voted in January 1837 against a resolution that attacked abolition societies "and the doctrines promulgated by them." They made a statement, however, designed to keep the antiabolitionists of their district happy, that their vote against the earlier measure was based on a difference over wording. "They [Stone and Lincoln] believe that the institution of slavery is founded on both injustice and bad policy; but that the promulgation of abolition doctrines tends rather to increase than to abate its evils." There was no doubt that Lincoln believed both propositions on slavery: that it was morally offensive yet constitutionally guaranteed. Because the abolitionists would not face that fact, it remained important to him politically to show that he had no truck with abolitionists.

The Long Nine went home again in late winter, proclaiming to their constituency the glorious fact that henceforth, through their good efforts, Springfield would be the state capital. Lincoln traveled home with some other legislators on horseback, and, stopping overnight in a village, they slept on the floor of a private house. One of his companions noticed that Lincoln was depressed. When his friend asked about it, Abe said that all the rest of them had something to look forward to. "But it isn't so with me. I am going home . . . without a thing in the world. I have drawn all my pay I got at Vandalia and have spent it all. I am in debt. . . . I don't know what to do."

Lincoln had had the same feelings in Vandalia, where things "I cannot account for, have conspired and gotten my spirit so low, that I feel I would rather be any place in the world than here." His depression might have been a failure of self-confidence, for he did have a future now. John T. Stuart, having just lost the partner in his practice, had suggested Lincoln come up to Springfield and join his law practice as a junior partner. Lincoln, having applied for and received a law license to practice in Sangamon County, was formally enrolled and permitted to charge fees on March 1, 1837. But since he had to show little more than a basic grasp of the law to get his license, he felt dubious about his capacity to succeed and was frightened by the prospect of Springfield.

So here is Lincoln in the spring of 1837: tortured in equal and abundant measure by self-doubt and ambition, ill-clothed, rough-mannered, hard up, possessed of his peculiarly American powers of articulation and charm, burdened by what now would be considered clinical depression, plagued by exultant vision, yearning for and terrified by women, raucous in joke telling, gifted in speech, abstinent in drink, profligate in dreams. No man ever entered Springfield, a town that would become his shrine, as tentative, odd-seeming, and daunted as Abraham Lincoln.

4

——————

THE NEW STATE CAPITAL, when Lincoln arrived, was a town of two thousand people, possessing many fine homes and business enterprises, owned generally by immigrants from Kentucky, often the children of slave-owning families. It had a debating and thespian society, and attracted visits by many leading political figures on their sweeps through the countryside. At first Lincoln felt uncomfortably excluded from all this urban activity, and wrote in a letter to the Kentuckian Mary Owens, "I am quite as lonesome here as I ever was anywhere in my life."

Lincoln's "hypo," brought out by the muddy streets of Springfield as by New Salem and Vandalia, and likely to incapacitate him at any time, has been hard for psychiatrists to diagnose. One famous study speaks of his mother fixation and his fear of the father, of narcissistic tendencies (not extending, of course, to his physical appearance) and a depressive temperament. Fortunately, in this case, the condition would be alleviated (though never cured) by his making friends in town, beginning to make real money, and maneuvering Mary Owens, after she visited him for a time in Springfield, into deciding that she could not trust his contradictory impulses toward marriage.

His best friend in Springfield was Joshua F. Speed, a young man of a Kentucky slaveholding family who owned what he described as "a large country store . . . everything that the country needed." Into Speed's store came the gangling Lincoln, and he priced bed furnishings. Finding that they would cost seventeen dollars, he confessed that he did not think he would earn enough to repay Speed (together with his other debts) in a reasonable time. Speed, admitting that "I never saw so gloomy, and melancholy a face," offered Lincoln accommodation in his own double bed above the store. In the nineteenth century it was not uncommon for men to share the same bed, even—in some boardinghouses—with males they did not know. Lincoln also stayed for a time with one William Butler and his wife. Fortunately, though so tall, he had a waiflike quality, and attracted many kindhearted friends, whom he always afterward honored and mentioned.

His hulking bedfellow, Speed, was quite a womanizer, "and kept a pretty woman in the city." One day Lincoln asked Speed, "Do you know where I can get *some?*" According to Speed, he sent Lincoln with a note to this woman, who appears to have been something of a prostitute. Lincoln and the girl stripped and were in bed before Lincoln remembered to ask about the price. The girl told him five dollars. Lincoln declared he could afford to pay her only three dollars, and the girl said she would trust him for the rest, but Lincoln declared he had other debts to meet, and rose and clothed himself again. As he left, according to Speed's secondhand telling of the encounter, the girl said, "You are the most conscientious man I ever saw." Speed would say generally that Lincoln's characteristic mood was one of sadness, but his face could suddenly brighten, and he would become radiant and glowing.

Congressman Stuart was frequently absent from the law office on national affairs, so that Lincoln was able to get practical experience and make a reasonable living—much of it out of trespass, nonpayment, slander, divorce, and property matters. His earnings were generally about eight hundred dollars per year, and, having earlier spent his savings as a legislator in Vandalia on two town lots in Springfield, he was now able to buy two more, and continued to reduce his debt.

The Sangamon County Circuit Court sat in Springfield only two weeks of the year, and so Lincoln and even Stuart himself were forced out on the road to follow the judges of the Eighth Judicial Circuit, and to take cases in the rustic courts on the circuit's sittings. Between the society of other young men at the back of Speed's store, in the Young Men's Lyceum, and elsewhere, and the company of other lawyers on circuit, Lincoln all at once had a rich social life and once more attracted loyal friends. It was the men he met as a lawyer on circuit who would one day help guarantee his ascent to the fabulously remote presidency. One of these was his future partner Stephen T. Logan. Another, Judge David Davis, claimed that Lincoln was at his happiest on the circuit, in the company of other lawyers, arguing with "sledgehammer logic" and pursuing his economical, logical arguments. He showed an extraordinary capacity for memory, for people's names, for the history of places, for dates.

Lincoln also had some of the talents that have been associated with less seemly areas of American law. Involved in a case on behalf of a widow and her son against another lawyer who had, in Lincoln's view, improperly acquired title to the family's land, Lincoln helped his client along by publishing a series of letters on the matter, attacking the other attorney and signing himself "Sampson's Ghost." Lincoln brought a youthful excess to these supposedly anonymous letters. The tactics were not uncommon in the legal or political profession—they had been used against Lincoln himself—but in this case the letters achieved nothing. When the other lawyer died, the matter was still unresolved, and the land passed to his heirs.

Despite Abraham's growing reputation, one Springfield lawyer declared, "In the light of subsequent events it sounds queer enough, but the fact is we considered ourselves a 'tony' crowd, and that Lincoln, although an extremely clever and well-liked fellow, was hardly up to our standard of gentility." And one of the motives Lincoln had offered Mary Owens not to marry him was, "[T]here is a great deal [of] flourishing about in carriages here, which it would be your doom to see without sharing in it."

A number of young women found Lincoln clumsy. One said, "L. could not hold a lengthy Conversation with a lady— was not sufficiently Educated & intelligent in the female line to do so." Calling on a girl named Anna Rodney, he knocked on her door, and outraged the member of the family who opened it by asking, "Is Miss Rodney handy?" This was considered a dé-classé inquiry.

In 1837 there was a run on American banks, caused by a col-lapse of British markets. The Jacksonian Democrats blamed it on the very nature of banks, and the way the American econ-omy was following the pernicious example of the European market system. A collapse certainly seemed to threaten Lin-coln's "American System" ideology. The economic anxieties of the year heightened tensions between pro- and antiabolition-ists. North Carolina and Georgia offered a reward of five thou-

sand dollars for the head of the famous Massachusetts abolitionist William Lloyd Garrison. There were race riots in a number of Northern cities, and in Illinois an abolitionist editor, the
Reverend Elijah Lovejoy, who would become in time a hearty
supporter of Lincoln, was attacked by a mob who shot him and
dumped his printing press in the Mississippi. Lincoln registered
his outrage in a speech before the Young Men's Lyceum. He
saw the danger of great internal fury arising from the issue. He
feared that the pressures would cause people to lose their at-
tachment to government, and if that happened, said Abraham
prophetically, "men of sufficient talent and ambition will not be
wanting to seize the opportunity, strike the blow, and overturn
that fair fabric, which for the last half century has been the
fondest hope for the lovers of freedom throughout the world."

In that spirit Lincoln ran again for the state legislature in
1838, and his former mentor Stuart ran yet again for Congress,
his opponent being the five-foot-four, thunderously eloquent
and powerful Stephen Douglas, the Little Giant. Douglas had
worked to transform the Democratic Party in the northwest
into a modern political machine that got out the vote and knew
how to use patronage. He had by now served in the statehouse
and been registrar of the Springfield land office. Four years
younger than Lincoln, he was considered by his party a fit candidate for Congress.

But Lincoln was reelected for Sangamon County, and Stuart won the savage fight, which frequently came to blows, with
Douglas.

In the economic crisis the Whigs of Springfield stuck to the
scheme of internal improvements, even though the ten million
dollars raised to pay for them was generating a crippling inter-

est bill. As leader of the Whigs, Lincoln suggested that the Federal government sell all the public land in Illinois to the government of Illinois for a cost of twenty-five cents per acre. The state government would then resell it at a minimum of $1.25, and thus obliterate its debts. The plan got nowhere, however, and by 1839 the governor called a special session of the assembly to deal with the crisis.

The leading wealthy Whigs of Springfield were called the Junto. John T. Stuart was certainly a member, and so was his cousin from Kentucky, Ninian Edwards, and his wife, Elizabeth. Ninian and Elizabeth Edwards lived on a hill in one of Springfield's grandest homes, and under his friend Stuart's aegis, Lincoln began attending social events there. Ninian found his fellow Whig a "mighty rough man," but tolerated him for his political usefulness. It was at the Edwardses' in late 1839 that Lincoln met Elizabeth Edwards's younger sister, a small, pert, intense, lively young woman named Mary Todd, of whom her brother-in-law said, "Mary could make a bishop forget his prayers." Mary certainly gave Abraham pause.

Mary was twenty-one, and her father was a Kentucky grandee, Robert Todd, plantation owner and slaveholder. Her mother had died in childbirth when Mary was seven, and Mary Todd would always have an orphan's questing edginess and insecurity. Things were made worse when her father remarried—to a woman Mary found cold and judgmental—and so in the summer of 1839 she had been delighted to move to Springfield, Illinois, taking up permanent abode in the Edwards household. She had been well educated, could speak French, and seems to have attracted a number of interested males. "Speed's grey suit, Harrison's blues, Lincoln's Lincoln green have gone to dust," she wrote to a friend, indicating how she played men off against one another. The Little Giant, the Democrat, Stephen Douglas, also very nearly proposed to Mary Todd, though Mary would say later that she liked him merely "well enough," and would rhapsodize about Lincoln's superiority to Douglas—that intellectually he towered over Douglas "just as he does physically." A widower, lawyer, and state legislator named Edwin Webb was a suitor, too.

In the Springfield courthouse on a cold day in November 1839, Mary Todd attended an event at which both Lincoln and Douglas were to speak "on the Politics of the Time and the Condition of the Country." Lincoln of course spoke of the validity of the state bank, which had recently had such a shake, and on methods to fund ongoing improvements. He was disappointed with his performance, and Stephen Douglas, he believed, had outshone him politically and perhaps as a suitor. But Elizabeth Edwards began to notice that her sister particularly liked Lincoln. "I have happened in a room where they were sitting often enough, and Mary led the conversation."

There was a political excitement to their odd courtship. The Whig candidate for the presidency in 1840 was William Henry Harrison, who had been chosen over the founding genius of the Whigs, Henry Clay. The Democratic candidate was the incumbent president, Martin Van Buren. Lincoln stumped the county and even went to Missouri to speak for Harrison, and he also saw fashionable young Mary and her best friend, Mercy Levering, crowding into the offices of the *Sangamo Journal* to get the latest news of the campaign and to pick up on the furious political atmosphere. Lincoln, of course, campaigned for himself for the state legislature while campaigning for the Whig presidential candidate, and on one occasion tied Stephen A. Douglas in knots over Van Buren's attitude toward Negro suffrage, to the point that the Little Giant snatched the evidence out of Lincoln's hand and hurled it into the crowd.

One Democrat provoked him by painting him as a representative of the aristocracy of the Whigs. Lincoln said that while his accuser was riding in a fine carriage, wearing his kid gloves, he himself "was a poor boy hired on a flatboat at $8 a month, and had only one pair of breeches . . . if you know the nature of buckskin when wet and dried by the sun, they would shrink and mine kept shrinking until they left for several inches my legs bare between my Socks and the lower part of my breeches. . . . If you call this aristocracy, I plead guilty to the charge."

Mary Todd and Abraham both hesitated at the idea of marriage. He was now making between fifteen hundred and two thousand dollars a year, with an additional one hundred to three hundred as a legislator. But if he lost clients, or lost the election, his income could suddenly fall. The fear of having caught syphilis from a prostitute and passing it on to a respectable wife, and fathering defective children, was still strong, if unfounded in his case. This was at the time not an unjustifiable fear, since it is claimed that more than 50 percent of nineteenth-century men contracted a form of venereal disease at one stage or another of their sexual history.

For her part Mary Todd realized that she would sacrifice many civil and legal rights when she married, and she had been so relishing her freedom in her sister's household that she wondered if she should surrender it. Elizabeth warned her too that "she and Mr. Lincoln were not suitable . . . they had no feelings alike." Mary Todd was well polished, whereas he still shocked polite Springfield society by wearing rough Conestoga boots into parlors, and on one occasion when entering a party cried, "Oh boys, how clean these girls look!"

According to Speed, too, Lincoln wasn't happy with his engagement, "not entirely satisfied that his *heart* was going with his hand." Some people say that Lincoln "fell desperately in love" with another Edwards relative, Matilda Edwards. There is evidence that he might have confessed this love to Mary and asked for and received her release. Friends now saw that his conscience troubled him dreadfully, and Speed felt bound to remove all razors from his room, along with knives and other sharp objects. By the end of January 1841, Lincoln confessed himself "the most miserable man living. If what I feel were equally distributed in the whole human family, there would not be one cheerful face on the earth." One friend described Lincoln as "having two catfits and a Duck fit." Lincoln was also distracted at the time because his old friend Speed had sold his store and was about to move back to Kentucky, while Stuart, reelected to Congress, had suggested an end to his law partnership with Lincoln.

Mary was tormented herself but not so fundamentally as Lincoln. Her suitors still fluttered around her. She was not socially incapacitated, and was now relieved of any premarriage anxieties. She found the summer slow and dreary, however, since many of her friends had left town. In letters to them she maintained a generous attitude to Lincoln, and hoped he would get over his melancholia. It says something about her that she was convinced of Lincoln's potential, even as many of her associates shook their heads over his apparently bumpkin qualities.

In the spring he signed a new partnership, with Stephen Logan, a small man with wiry red hair and an alto voice, who, like Lincoln, put little emphasis on the way he dressed. Logan was also a compulsive whittler, and would sometimes, if not provided quickly with wood, start in on people's furniture. The partnership was a bright point in a dismal spring, during which Lincoln's service as a state assemblyman was drawing to an end. The Whigs did not nominate him for reelection, nor did he particularly want them to. The public works program, for which he had stood all these years, had been much reduced in scope, the state had defaulted on its debts, and the state bank of Illinois, supposed engine of the state's wealth, had been dissolved.

Having sold up and gone back to Kentucky, Speed insisted that Lincoln visit the family's plantation in Kentucky that summer. It was Lincoln's first experience of a plantation house, of the opulence based upon the peculiar institution of slavery. In his languid recuperation from the "hypo," he was tended by the Speeds' slaves. On the way back up the Ohio with Speed on a steamboat, Lincoln encountered a coffle, a chained line of twelve slaves, "like so many fish upon a trot-line." These men had been taken from their families in Kentucky, Lincoln had learned on inquiry, and were being shipped for sale elsewhere. Lincoln would later claim that the memory of this line of flesh-as-property "was a continual torment to me."

Down in Kentucky, Joshua Speed married, and Lincoln began to interrogate him on how marriage suited him. The questions Lincoln asked in letters were curiously and obsessively framed: "Are you now, in feeling as well as in judgement, glad you are married as you are?" Speed shared these questions with his young wife, who found them impudent. But they serve as an index to Lincoln's neurotic bewilderment.

At last, in 1842, a mutual friend brought Abraham and Mary together again, asking them to be, at least, friends to each other. Dr. Anselm Henry, the notable Springfield physician to whom Lincoln had taken the problem of his "hypo" the year before, also acted as go-between. At some stage Lincoln asked Mary whether she believed he had incurred any obligation to marry her, and Mary—or Molly, as he called her—did not miss the opportunity to let him know she believed he had.

5

ALL AT ONCE it was another election year, and Lincoln campaigned for the Whigs. As part of his service, he took up the issue of a colorful little Irishman named James Shields, Democratic auditor for Illinois, who was trying to undermine further the tottering state bank. To the Irish in America, Shields was a national hero and a defiant refugee from British oppression. Shields announced that the state would no longer accept paper currency as payment for debts, and only gold and silver coin would be accepted for tax payments. Lincoln rightly considered that these decisions would reduce the economy of Illinois to a primitive condition, and so he began to plant in the *Sangamo Journal* a series of letters supposedly written by a naive widow named Rebecca, and designed to satirize Shields.

Out of both political passion and passion for Lincoln, Mary and a friend took over the writing of the series. In their joint amusement at Shield's embarrassment, Abraham and Mary Todd grew closer. Mary managed to compose a Rebecca letter that particularly stung Shields. When Shields challenged whoever the writer of the Rebecca letters was, Lincoln accepted responsibility for all of them, and Shields proposed a duel. One morning that autumn the two contestants and their supporters slipped over the river into Missouri, where dueling was still legal. Perhaps satirically, Lincoln had proposed broadswords as the weapons, but it seems that their seconds and friends talked both of them out of the potentially bloody fight anyhow. Lincoln was afterward embarrassed by the incident, but Mary, from dueling Kentucky, was impressed at the risk he had taken for her.

During that year's electoral struggle, Lincoln, to whom politics was still life's chief sport, gave Mary a curious present—a list of election returns in the last three legislative races! She took it in the spirit in which it was offered, and wrapped it in a pink ribbon. Six weeks after the contest with Shields, on a day of freezing rain, Mary Todd and Abraham Lincoln were married in the parlor of the Edwards home. Mary was now twenty-three years old, a small but fetching firebrand. Many friends, nonetheless, doubted the sincerity of this wedding. John Todd Stuart, Mary's cousin, feared that "the marriage of Lincoln to Miss Todd was a policy match all round," giving Lincoln an entrée into the centers of Whig power. Lincoln's best man recalled that he "looked and acted as if he was going to a slaughter." Indeed, the lawyer Billy Herndon claimed that "Lincoln self-sacrificed himself rather than be charged with dishonor." Interestingly, like other poor boys marrying above themselves, he invited no one from his family to attend the event.

By now the bridegroom had his eye on representing the Seventh District in Congress. The bride never wavered from a determined belief in her husband's talent and a profound though jealous respect for him. And, although they began their marriage in rented rooms in the Globe Tavern, Lincoln's new partnership with Logan did well, helped along by the numbers of bankruptcies that needed to be processed. Joshua Speed

bought up many foreclosed houses and lots, which were processed through Lincoln's practice.

After their first winter of married life, Lincoln went back on
the road, traveling around the circuit with other lawyers, ac-
cepting cases as they went. Mary was bored—having to eat at a
communal table in a boardinghouse was a comedown for her.
By then it was apparent that she was pregnant as well, and so
she suffered a large part of the malaise of pregnancy with Lincoln away in his preferred environment, chatting in rural inns
with fellow Whig lawyers about the tragedy that, after they had
worked so hard to get President Harrison elected, he had gone
and died, leaving his Democratic vice president, John Tyler, in
the seat of power, where he pursued all the old cramped, anti-
tariff, antibank, and pro-Southern policies Lincoln disliked.

Back from circuit in August 1843, Lincoln celebrated the
birth of his first child, Robert Todd Lincoln. It was now Lincoln's turn to have a son who, as well as resembling the Todds
closely, would in temperament be something of a stranger to
him. The Lincolns moved out of the Globe to rent a cottage on
Fort Street, and would soon buy a house at H and Jackson, a respectable one-and-a-half-story frame structure that cost Lincoln twelve hundred dollars and where they would live until he
achieved the presidency.

Abraham would prove, by the standards of his time, an
overindulgent father to all his children, and even to Robert,
whom Herndon would later dismiss as "a Todd and not a Lincoln." But it has to be said that Abraham had relief from do-
mesticity when he went on circuit, and Mary had none. Mary
too was indulgent, but in another sense: in a fraught manner in-

terspersed with outbursts of anger. The house sometimes overwhelmed her. She had but one servant, and the nature of domestic life as wife of a young lawyer with no independent means and, of course, no slaves shocked her and made her anxious. Her fear of poverty would become a monomania, plaguing her for the rest of her life, but it often manifested itself in fits of alternating extravagance (especially when it came to clothes and furnishings) and frenzied cheeseparing. She had an unpredictable temper—a trait not unknown in the Todd family—and neighbors overheard some of the fights, in which Mary's stridency would be interspersed with Lincoln's desperately appeasing, "Now there, Mother." At tenderer moments he called her, "My child wife, my Molly," and yet he often found that the easiest way to deal with her was to take to the streets or to his office. A friend of Lincoln's described her as a "she-devil." Her tantrums "vexed & harrowed the soul out of that good man."

But his distant and abstracted nature frustrated her, and Mary must often have chided him about the limitations of his success, for she told a friend, "If Mr. Lincoln should happen to die, his spirit will never find me living outside the boundaries of a slave state." And since he still rode the circuit six months out of the year, Mary was often on her own, and oppressed by fears about her children, which some called morbid.

Now that she had her own house, and despite her bemoaning the lack of slaves, Mary sturdily insisted on doing much of her own work, when by contrast her sister, Elizabeth Edwards, had two Irish-born servants and a laborer, as well as two slaves from the Todd house in Kentucky (and thus of uncertain status as to whether they were bond or free). Sometimes Mary's tantrums drove away even the help she had. One servant would later complain, "I was never so unhappy in my life as while living with her." Servants could find Mary unexpectedly generous, though, suddenly as energetic in generosity as she had been, just a minute or two before, in shrillness.

The servant who lasted longest was an Irishwoman, Katherine Gordon, although Mary wrote to her half sister Emilie: "If some of you Kentuckians had to deal with 'the wild Irish,' as we householders are sometimes called to do, the South would certainly elect Mr. Fillmore next time." Millard Fillmore was one of the leaders of the Know-Nothings, passionately anti-Irish and anti-Catholic. It can be said for Lincoln that although it was quite fashionable for Whigs to slam the Irish, given that they were electoral fodder for the Democrats, he never stooped to do so.

Late in 1844 Logan sought to dissolve the partnership, since he wanted to form another with his son. Lincoln intended to carry on on his own, but looked around for an assistant and chose Billy Herndon, who had clerked for him and who was genial company. Herndon, one day to write a controversial biography of his friend, was a loquacious, well-dressed young man in his mid-twenties. He was a freethinker, which appealed to Abe, and a bohemian boozer, which Abe wasn't. He also possessed considerable power among young Whigs. A voracious reader, he took a great number of liberal magazines from Britain and the East, subscribing as well to Horace Greeley's *New-York Tribune*. Lincoln would sometimes ask him to give digests of the ideas he had encountered in recent books, something Herndon was willing to do. In an age of advancing Victorian prudery, he would later be attacked for indelicately recording that Lincoln told him, "My Mother was a bastard—was the daughter of a nobleman, So called of Virginia. . . . All that I am and hope ever to be I get from my Mother—good bless her—Did you ever notice that bastards are generally smarter—shrewder & more intellectual than others? Is it because it is stolen?"

Billy Herndon always sided with Lincoln in his home problems, and called the Lincoln household "domestic *hell* on earth." It was, said Herndon again, "an ice cave."

But then, perhaps understandably, Lincoln did frequently absent himself from that cave. In 1844 he stumped the state and rode into Indiana to address rallies for his political paragon, Henry Clay, Whig champion and candidate for the presidency. But a protégé of Andrew Jackson, James Knox Polk, took the White House. The previous year, at a party convention in Pekin, Illinois, Lincoln had put himself forward as congressional candidate, but a cousin of Mary's, John J. Hardin, received the nomination. Lincoln did, however, manage to broker a deal by which the Seventh Congressional District would rotate between Hardin, Lincoln's close friend Edward Baker, and Lincoln himself. (Edward Baker, after whom the Lincolns would name their second son, was a state senator who often appeared on political rostrums with a pet eagle.) Lincoln could look forward with some certainty to being a candidate in 1846 and taking his seat in Congress the following year.

Even before Polk was inaugurated, the United States acquired Texas as a slaveholding state. Under the Missouri Compromise of 1820, slavery could not exist north of thirty six degrees thirty minutes latitude. The Southern Democrats, therefore, pursued a policy of encouraging annexation of territory south of the compromise line. They dreamed not only of Texas but of Central America and Cuba, whose incorporation as future slave states would perpetuate the balance between slave and free jurisdictions and ensure that the peculiar institution spread and flourished. It was for fear that border and land disputes in Texas would cause the U.S. Army to be unjustly employed to conquer more territory for slavery's domain that Lincoln campaigned so much for Henry Clay, who—though himself a Kentucky slaveholder—saw the spread of the slave empire as pernicious, and a gradual end to the institution of slavery as inevitable.

As, to the horror of such Whigs as Lincoln, the American army marched into Mexico, Lincoln and Billy Herndon moved into new premises across the public square from the courthouse. It was an office that quickly took on an increasing look of disarray, Lincoln even having a parcel of documents tied with string and classified with the words: "When you can't find it anywhere else, look into this." Apple seeds and orange rinds from Abraham's profuse fruit eating littered the floor. Herndon was a newshound, so that the floor was also strewn with pages of broadsheets. To add to the eccentricity of the office, Lincoln filed papers in his stovepipe hat, a habit he had picked up during his time as a postmaster-surveyor in New Salem. He made frequent use of the sofa, which was too small for his long body, so that his upper body would lie on it and the lower would be extended over a number of chairs. Thus he would lie under heaps of newspapers.

The partners got along, but Mary could not tolerate Herndon and never had him in the house. She learned that he had described her as a serpent, and though he claimed he had intended it as a reference to her gracefulness, she never forgave him. He would ultimately, in his famous biography, give her other and more concrete reasons for dislike.

Though Mary's distant cousin John Hardin tried again to get the nomination for the Seventh Congressional District in 1846, Lincoln lobbied hard as he moved around the state on circuit, and managed to outmaneuver the man. It was the year his second son, Edward, was born, and having been elected, Lincoln suddenly confessed that the honor did not please him as much as he had expected. He was perhaps daunted by balancing the interests of his sons, his law practice, and his party. But Mary was delighted. She intended to go with him to Washington for the next congressional session in 1847.

When the family set out for the national capital in the fall of 1847, they intended to travel by way of Kentucky to visit Mary's beloved father and not-so-cherished stepmother, Betsey Todd. Betsey had never met Mary's husband or children. It was a testing journey for the couple, the thirty-eight-year-old congressman, his twenty-six-year-old wife, their four-year-old son, Robert, and infant Eddie already beginning to suffer from the onset of tuberculosis. They took the stagecoach to Alton on the Mississippi, then one steamer down to Cairo, another up the Ohio to Carrollton, a third down the Kentucky River to Frankfort, and then went on by train into Lexington. This part of the journey occupied ten fretful days. When the visit home was over, they went on by stage, steamer, and rail into the Shenandoah Valley and so to Washington.

Washington was an imperfect capital, its great civic buildings only partially completed, its roads dusty in summer and mired in winter, its environment malarial, its water supply dangerous to health, and its accommodations overpriced. Dickens had recently satirized the capital as "a small piece of country which has taken to drinking, and has quite lost itself." He complained of its "spacious avenues that begin in nothing and lead nowhere. . . ."

Many legislators lived in "messes," corps of like-minded congressmen and senators, in such hotels as Brown's or in boardinghouses. Some of the wealthier were able to rent houses. The humble Lincolns took a room in Mrs. Sprigg's boardinghouse, across from the Capitol, on the site of what is now the Library of Congress. Mrs. Sprigg's place was a favorite haunt of Whig congressmen of antislavery stripe. Only a minority of wives accompanied their husbands to Washington for the congressional sessions, and they were often the wives of powerful plantation owners. Mary was the only wife among the ten legislators Mrs. Sprigg accommodated in her house at that time. A number of the guests thought that both Mary and Abe indulged Robert too much, and they were disturbed by Eddie's crying. And although Mary Todd would enjoy shopping in Washington, in the boutiques and bookshops of Pennsylvania Avenue, and visiting the sights, such as the unfinished Washington Memorial and the Museum of the Patent Office, the bitter Washington winter kept her increasingly indoors and restive. The children caught illnesses. The present day Ellipse, behind the Capitol, was then a putrid and infectious swamp.

After Lincoln's session Mary went back to stay at her father's house in Lexington. She was not above jovially threatening that if Abraham did not come to see her there soon, she might take up again with Mr. Webb, her old suitor. In an age of foreshortened lives, she did contemplate the possibility of future husbands, and told her half sister Emilie that next time she wanted one rich enough to take her to Europe. She returned to Washington for the second session of Abraham's term and then, as Lincoln exerted his merely moderate degree of influence in Washington, went back to Springfield and stayed at the Globe with her two sons, because their house was still rented out.

Abraham himself liked the boardinghouse and Washington. He played bowls in the lane behind Mrs. Sprigg's and in the bowling alley south of the Capitol. He took his wife to the Olympian Theatre and Caruso's Saloon, with its so-called Ethiopian serenaders, who performed comedy and minstrel songs in blackface. The Lincolns also attended events at the White House (the President's House, as it was then more commonly called). They were of course present for President Polk's New Year's reception for 1848. By then Lincoln and other Whigs were in polite but passionate opposition to Polk over what they saw as the American intrusion into Mexican territory, and the cancellation of internal improvement projects.

In these matters, as in all his political beliefs, Lincoln followed a coherent political philosophy, much of it influenced by the very Calvinism he had already rejected. He believed, as he said, in the "Doctrine of Necessity"—that is, "that the human mind is impelled to action, or held in rest by some power, over which the mind itself has no control." In political terms this meant that he believed "all human actions were caused by motives, and at the bottom of motives were self." This fatalism explained to his satisfaction why Southern advocates of slavery were no better or worse than Northerners—slavery was upheld by the motives of *self* inherent in the Southern system, and thus Southern interests tried to expand its reign to new territories. The North's desire for tariffs was similarly driven. The difference was of course one of morality—tariffs would be a morally laudable outcome of the doctrine of necessity; slavery was not.

His own escape from subsistence farming was based on this doctrine of necessity, and as he had wished to be free, so too must the slaves. "I used to be a slave," he had said in an early speech, and recognizing a friend from Offut's flatboat in the crowd, continued, "There is my old friend John Rowan. He used to be a slave, but he has made himself free, and I used to be a slave, and now I am so free that they let me practice law."

Democrats such as Douglas saw wage labor as a form of slavery that created a noxious dependency between the worker and the employer. Increasingly, throughout the next decade and a half, Democrats would point to the conditions of Northern industrial, railroad, and navigation canal workers as far more severe than those under the more beneficent institutions of slavery. In slavery the plantation owner had an investment in the individual slave and thus had a motive to treat him or her well. Capital could use up and kill the laborer without any compunction.

Lincoln, however, saw wage labor as a mere way station on the ascent to the status and decent affluence that characterized his own life. There was no need for anyone to remain a wage-laborer indefinitely. Necessity would drive a man through enlightened self-interest to become an employer himself. Like many a man who had remade himself, he falsely considered that any laborer had the same gift thus to transform himself, to become a merchant or a lawyer or at least an employer of other labor. He was sometimes impatient when relatives were too feckless to shake themselves free of their rustic helplessness. For example, his stepbrother John D. Johnston wrote to him for a loan of eighty dollars to cover various cash debts he'd incurred. Lincoln accused Johnston of being "lazy . . . what I propose is, that you shall go to work, 'tooth and nails' for somebody who will give you money for it." A man who worked for wages this year could afford in the next to "work for himself afterward, and finally to hire men to work for him!" As an incentive, however, Lincoln did offer to match Johnston dollar for dollar.

There was one answer to the poverty of the cities, but it was one the Southern and Northern Democrats would not vote for—a homestead act that would open up allotments in the new territories to free occupation by the slum dwellers and ill-paid artisans of the cities, and to the poor farmers of the East. These new territories would be run, according to the Whig ideal, not on the basis of the dark drudgery of Lincoln's boyhood but on that of the newest agricultural knowledge, disseminated by agricultural colleges in their midst. Yet every time such measures would be proposed, Southern interests voted them down, for fear that the new territories would become hotbeds of abolition, and that free land would undermine land values.

Yet despite his moral contempt for slavery and its advocates, Lincoln's impatience with abolitionists still prevailed. He considered them to have cost Henry Clay the presidency in 1844 by frightening people with all their of talk of imminent crisis and black-white equality. In fact Lincoln had sometimes acted as counsel for slave owners, such as the Kentuckian Robert Matson, in pursuit of their property rights. In 1843 Matson had purchased a farm in Illinois and brought a group of slaves over the Ohio River for planting and harvest. They included the slave wife and children of Matson's black overseer, Bryant, who was a freedman. When Matson's common-law wife had an argument with the slave wife, Jane, Matson threatened to send her and her children down South for resale to a cotton plantation. The Bryants sought the help of two abolitionists to fund a challenge, but Matson hired Lincoln, who argued that Matson had clearly stated his intention to limit the service of Jane and her children in Illinois to seasonal labor only, under the Illinois transit laws. The Illinois Supreme Court found that Jane Bryant had been in Illinois for a continuous two years and declared her free.

Since the Constitution gave slavery legal sanction, only a constitutional amendment could alter it, and this could be achieved only with the consent of the South, which obviously would not be forthcoming. The fortunate reality, thought Lincoln, was that the institution was doomed—it would, like the subsistence farming of his childhood, be rendered obsolete. Like Henry Clay, Lincoln and many of the Whigs with whom he played bowls in the back alley believed that the future and just liberation of the slaves would be a prelude to colonizing them back to Liberia or to Central America.

But through the war against Mexico, the South and its friends were attempting to ward off the withering of their institution by expanding it into new territories. As a congressman Lincoln rose in the House to offer some "spot resolutions" attacking President Polk, but before he was allowed to go to the rostrum, Mexico City had been captured by the United States. Lincoln's resolutions attacking the war were depicted as disloyalty to the victorious army, and at Democratic rallies Abe was lambasted as "spotty" Lincoln. By late 1848 Lincoln was caught in a quandary by his opposition to the war. The Whigs wanted their candidate to be a war hero—Zachary Taylor, with whom Lincoln had once campaigned in the Black Hawk War. No one was particularly delighted with Taylor, but his party could see that he was eminently electable, despite the problem for the New England vote that he was a slaveholder.

Horace Greeley of the *New-York Tribune* noticed Lincoln's term in Congress to the extent of saying that he was a strong but practical enemy of slavery. Toward the end of the Thirtieth Congress, in January 1849, Lincoln announced that he had a proposal for abolishing slavery in the District of Columbia. It involved compensation of the district's slave owners for the "full value" of their property. It went nowhere.

Indeed, he had not been a particularly impressive congressman, and was not satisfied with his own performance. But then, it was hard work for a one-term congressman. Members had no offices and worked at their cramped desks like so many schoolchildren. Lincoln's desk was, of course, at the back of the chamber. He sought solace from his insignificant presence in the chamber by spending much time in the Congressional Library, which was then located within the Capitol itself. He was able to take books home to Mrs. Sprigg's, even books from the founding collection of the library—Jefferson's personal library.

At the end of his term, Lincoln did not return home at once but went on the campaign trail, campaigning for Zachary Taylor. He even confessed—blasphemy in his eyes—that Henry Clay would have had no hope as the Whig candidate. He went to the Whig National Convention in Philadelphia, though he was not a delegate, and he worked at Whig national headquarters. It was obvious to some that he hoped for an appointment out of all this—he had sniffed glory, had not possessed it, but did not yet wish to leave the field. He hoped to have an Illinois ally, a relative of Mary's, appointed commissioner of the General Land Office, but when he was told that his friend had proved unappointable, he tried for the post himself. This fact did not much improve his relationship with the Edwardses back in Springfield. Yet, Zachary Taylor having been elected president, he was generally disappointed that "not one recommended by me has yet been appointed to anything, little or big, except a few who had no opposition." In the late spring of 1849, Mary herself took up Lincoln's cause by writing to President Taylor, signing her letters in his name. But Lincoln lost the contest, and was offered instead the secretaryship and ultimately the governorship of Oregon Territory. As one friend said, "Mary would not consent to go out there." Lincoln was not enthusiastic either. Should the Lincolns make the trip by sea, the most feasible way, Eddie's health might well be further imperiled by the journey: Two children of the incumbent governor had died on the journey around Cape Horn.

The Whig nominee to succeed Lincoln in the seat in Congress, Stephen Logan, Mary's cousin, would be defeated by the Democrats. Some blamed the defeat not on Logan's personal unpopularity but on Lincoln's passionate opposition to the successfully concluded war against Mexico.

Returning to Springfield, Lincoln told Billy Herndon that he was "politically dead." Without politics he had time for family and reading. "I am reading books again, *The Iliad* and *Odyssey*. You ought to read it. He has a grip and knows how to tell a story."

6

IT WAS JUST AS WELL that Lincoln had time for the domestic sphere, because on February 1, 1850, after fifty-two days of a pitiable respiratory struggle, Eddie died. Child deaths were common enough for books of etiquette to advise Christian mothers how to behave when they lost their children. *The Mother's Assistant* described a bad mother as saying, "I cannot lose my child, I cannot. She is so bright and promising," whereas a good mother "leaned on the Almighty and meekly bowed her head to earthly things."

The latter advice was untenable for Mary Todd. She was demented by grief, even though the new pastor of the First Presbyterian Church gave her such comfort that she changed her allegiance to its brand of Presbyterianism. In comforting each other, the Lincolns begot another child, who was born the following December. The boy, named William, proved to be an engaging and precocious child.

Lincoln knew that his father, Tom, had been ill in 1849—"attacken with a lesion of the Heart" according to Lincoln's stepbrother, John D. Johnston. When Thomas became fatally ill in the winter of 1850–51, Johnston again notified Abraham, who decided not to leave his wife, still ill from the birth of William, to visit his dying father. "If we could meet now, it is doubtful whether it would not be more painful than pleasant," Lincoln told Johnston. "At all events tell him to remember to call upon, and confide in, our great, and good, and merciful Maker." Thomas Lincoln died in January 1851, and Abraham did not attend the funeral or ever raise a monument over his father's grave.

In the vacuum left by Lincoln's failed political hopes, the law practice of Lincoln and Herndon flourished in the first half of the 1850s, and so, in its way, did the Lincoln family. Another boy, Thomas, was born in 1853, a fetching and affectionate child with a speech impediment, for whom Lincoln had a special weakness, nicknaming him "Tad" (tadpole). Tad was a prankster, and his tendency to mischief was enhanced by his father's leniency toward him and Willie. Lincoln could often be seen in the streets, towing Willie and Tad along in a little cart. Many Springfielders would consider them brats. Their father often took them to his law office, and while he spoke to clients, the two small boys "clamored over his legs, patted his cheeks, pulled his nose, and poked their fingers in his eyes, without causing reprimand or even notice." Herndon complained that the boys "would tear up the office, scatter the books, smash up pens, spill the ink and piss all over the floor. I have felt many, many a time that I wanted to wring their little necks." Herndon believed that "had they shit in Lincoln's hat and rubbed it on his boots, he would have laughed and thought it smart."

Mary was as ever more volatile with her boys, and she swung between indulgence and severity, sometimes spanking them fiercely and then becoming overwhelmed with guilt. Her moods might have accounted for their frequent presence in Lincoln's office when he was not on circuit.

Those days Lincoln found that he could reach most of the county seats in the Eighth Circuit by rail. And he was amused but delighted to find himself a mentor to younger lawyers, such as the Maine aristocrat Leonard Swett, who would become a Lincoln devotee and work for his election as president. Since his early days as a lawyer, Lincoln had grown to be more interested in reconciliation than in litigation. He had become, too, an expert on railroad matters, and represented the Illinois Central in such disputes as whether county authorities could tax a railroad. He similarly served the Tonica and Petersburg Railroad, the Alton & Sangamon, and the Ohio and Mississippi.

One particularly significant case of Lincoln's involved the Rock Island Railroad, which had built a rail bridge across the Mississippi into the new state of Iowa. In May 1856 a steamboat named the *Effie Afton,* struggling against eddies around the bridge pylons, crashed against one and caught fire. The owners sued the Rock Island Railroad. Lincoln saw this case as a struggle between East-West railroad transportation and the primacy of the North-South Mississippi, the preferred route of the Southern supremacists. Despite its early favors to him, the Mississippi was Slavery Way, whereas the East-West railways were Liberation Boulevard. Lincoln's defense of the railroad company in the Illinois Supreme Court was a triumph. He had done extensive groundwork—measuring distances around the bridge, discovering that one of the *Effie Afton*'s engines had been malfunctioning, and that the captain knew it had been before he tried to take it under the bridge. The jury was hung, and there would be appeals for many years, reaching the U.S. Supreme Court. But the bridge had survived, and Lincoln's reputation, in Illinois at least, was enhanced.

He also built up an expertise in patent cases, particularly those having to do with the flood of steam-powered agricultural machinery designs appearing on the market. (These too held out a promise of ending the human drudgery that had characterized his childhood.) In a case over the renowned McCormack Virginia Reaper, Lincoln was recruited to defend another inventor, John H. Manny, an Illinois man, against McCormack's accusation of patent infringement. The defense Lincoln and his colleague would raise was that McCormack was using an infringement suit to scare off the inventiveness and industry of others. The case moved on to Cincinnati, however, and a new lawyer, the stocky, pugnacious Edwin M. Stanton, joined the team. Stanton was already such a legal star that he wondered why they had bothered to bring in a "long-armed Ape" from Illinois. (He had, of course, no idea that he would one day serve very happily in the supposed simian's cabinet.) Lincoln had the gift of humility—it was one of the reasons he was beloved—and as best he could he sat and learned from Stanton, but was hurt by his daily contempt and hubris.

In the winter of 1854, there occurred in the Senate an event that would in the end propel Lincoln to national prominence. In the meantime it brought most luster to Stephen Douglas, by now the Little King of Illinois. Unlike Lincoln, Douglas had been no one-term Congressman. He had by now served three terms as a U.S. representative and had been a U.S. senator from Illinois since 1847. As one of the Democratic Party's most notable ideologues, he was sick of all the time the question of slavery was taking up in Congress, and the passions it unleashed. He proposed a new Nebraska Bill, designed to divide the vastness of Nebraska into two new territories, Nebraska and Kansas.

Within them the question of whether they would be slave or free would be decided by popular vote—a process Douglas called "popular sovereignty." The Missouri Compromise, which had until then banned slavery beyond the latitude of thirty-six degrees thirty minutes, was thus voided.

Lincoln was simply one politician among many who were appalled when this bill became the Kansas-Nebraska Act a few months later. Douglas's initiative brought Lincoln back to passionate participation in politics, since it violated a number of his profoundly held principles. He wanted the West to be a home for free white people. It would not be so if it became slave states. "Slave states are places for poor white people to remove from; not to remove to."

He achieved prominence in the opposition to the Kansas-Nebraska "popular sovereignty" act with a speech delivered by torchlight in Peoria in the fall of 1854. "Near eighty years ago," he said, "we began by declaring that all men are created equal; but now from that beginning we have run down to the other declaration, that for *some* men to enslave *others* is a 'sacred right of self-government.'" On a pragmatic level he pointed out that the self-interest of Northern laborers and settlers was opposed to the flooding of the market by Southerners, who could bring their slave labor north for indefinite periods and take employment away from whites.

The Peoria speech helped Lincoln again achieve the Whig nomination for a seat in the state legislature, but when elected he resigned the seat so that he could contest the nomination for the U.S. Senate, where he hoped to take a national part in the great fight against the extension of slavery inherent in the

Kansas-Nebraska issue. Illinois senators were at that stage elected indirectly by the members of the state house. Young, elegant Swett; the hefty Judge Davis, whom Lincoln knew from his life on the circuit; Ward Hill Lamon, who would one day guard Lincoln's life with his own; Stephen T. Logan, his former law partner—all converged on Springfield to drum up support for Lincoln among the legislators.

While Lincoln waited in his law office on February 8, 1855, Mary watched the balloting for the Senate seat from the gallery of the state legislature. Lincoln won the first ballot but was six votes short of victory. However, in negotiations, anti-Nebraska Democrats who had joined with anti-Nebraska Whigs to oppose Douglas, declared that they would never vote for Lincoln. Their support looked as if it would go to a Democrat, so Lincoln sent word from his office that he would withdraw and give his support to his fellow Whig Lyman Trumbull, an electable, urbane Yankee. The Lincoln team was devastated, and Mary would never forgive Trumbull or his wife, her former friend. Lincoln's loss brought on a sharp case of his "hypo." He did measure his own modest status against that of Douglas, triumphant in Washington, dominant in national affairs. And though Trumbull sought a great deal of help and advice from Lincoln, it was not enough to console Lincoln or to make Mary Lincoln forgive him.

The slavery issue had split the Whigs asunder, many Southern Whigs being pro-Nebraska—that is, pro–popular sovereignty. The question was whether Whigs should now join the free-soil, antislavery coalition called the Republican Party. But the Republican Party did not seem as strong as the American

Party—the party of the Know-Nothings—anti-Catholic, anti-Irish, and anti-immigrant in general, and Lincoln could not contemplate joining forces with Know-Nothing abolitionists.

> I do not perceive how any one professing to be sensitive to the wrongs of the negroes, can join in a league to degrade a class of white men. Our progress into degeneracy appears to be pretty rapid. As a nation, we began by declaring that *"All men are created equal."* We now practically read it *"All* men are created equal, *except negroes."* When the Know-Nothings get control, it will read, "All men are created equal, except negroes, *and foreigners, and catholics."* When it comes to this, I shall prefer emigrating to some country where they make no pretense of loving liberty—to Russia, for instance, where despotism can be taken pure, and without the base alloy of hypocrisy.

Meanwhile, proslavery invaders from Missouri rampaged into Kansas, attacking Free-Soilers. Ultimately they would attack and set fire to the free-soil capital of Lawrence, Kansas. But the Free-Soilers had their avatars of vengeance too. John Brown, the abolitionist zealot, went to Kansas with wagonloads of armaments to bring down God's vengeance on slavery.

Even as the Whigs split apart over the Kansas-Nebraska issue, so too did the Know-Nothings. Lincoln still remained a loyal Illinois Whig, and as such attended a convention at Bloomington, Illinois, in the spring of 1856, whose purpose was to make a coalition of all the anti-Nebraska forces in Illinois. This coalition found itself in accord with other such groupings throughout the North who called themselves Republicans. It seemed apparent to Lincoln that to participate in the broad fight of anti-Nebraska, of free-soil, one must be a member of the new organization. Lincoln thus became a Republican, and brought many other Illinois Whigs, including Billy Herndon and Stephen Logan, with him.

He gave the last speech at that Bloomington convention, and everyone said it was electrifying. Only some of its sentiments survive: "He was here ready to fuse with anyone who would unite with him to oppose the slave power."

The Republicans would indeed launch a national ticket in 1856. The Illinois Republican convention in Bloomington proposed Lincoln as a vice presidential candidate. The presidential nominee was John Charles Frémont, soldier, explorer, and former Democrat. Lincoln stayed home from the national convention in Philadelphia in June, but discovered that he received as many as 110 votes as vice presidential candidate (not nearly enough for the nomination, which went to William Dayton of New Jersey). Lincoln was secretly delighted at garnering so many delegates at the national level, though he joked, "There is a great man named Lincoln in Massachusetts, and he must be the one for whom the votes were cast."

Mary, a political woman and thus an oddity for her age, had no doubts that her husband was at last coming into his political inheritance. She nagged him about it, said Herndon, "like a toothache." "Nobody knows me," Lincoln would habitually assure her. But fierce Mary always responded, "They soon will."

Lincoln stumped around the state in support of Frémont, even traveling into Michigan for the purpose. He was a man for whom oratory was somewhere between an art form, a sport, and a drug. But the anti-Democrat vote was split between the Know-Nothing candidate, Millard Fillmore, whom Mary supported, and Frémont.

About the elderly Democratic candidate, James Buchanan, there hung an air of fatherly calm, and people trusted him to cool down the passions of the era. Their hopes would prove illusory, but Buchanan won the presidency, his very lack of fiery rhetoric and his apparently appeasing air being his chief political assets. Thinking about the reason for the Republicans' defeat, Lincoln believed it was that people thought Republicans were in favor of amalgamating the black and white races. He fiercely defended himself and fellow Republicans from any such charge.

It was that winter of political unease, after the high promise of his 110 vice presidential votes in the autumn, which caused him, in the spirit of the "hypo," again to compare himself unfavorably with Stephen A. Douglas. He remembered when they had first met in Vandalia twenty-two years before. They had both been ambitious, but, "with *me,* the race of ambition has been a failure—a flat failure; with *him* it has been one of splendid success. His name fills the nation; and is not unknown, even in foreign lands."

He hungered to have influence on a national level. His best hope to redress this imbalance between himself and the Little Giant would come in opposing Douglas for the U.S. Senate in 1858. He had won Mary from Douglas long ago. Now he wanted to take the Senate podium away from him.

7

TWO DAYS AFTER Buchanan was inaugurated in 1857, another blow against freedom was struck by the Supreme Court. Dred Scott was a middle-aged slave whose owner had taken him into the northern part of the Louisiana Purchase. After eight years in the Illinois and Wisconsin Territories, and the death of his master, he brought a lawsuit on the basis that his long residence on free soil made him a free man. The Chief Justice of the Supreme Court, Roger Taney, was determined to have none of that. Seven of the nine justices rejected Scott's suit, on the grounds that blacks could never be considered citizens under the Constitution, and that the federal government had no power to affect the status or the movement of black property. The Declaration of Independence did not cover blacks, who were "so far inferior that they had no rights which the white man was bound to respect."

Taney and Buchanan both believed that this would put an end to the slavery debate, but even Democrats like Stephen Douglas were appalled by the decision, since it went so much further than the idea of popular sovereignty as to make the latter—the idea that people of a state could vote to accept or refuse slavery—irrelevant. No territorial legislature could decide to exclude slavery! Douglas was horrified when Buchanan decided to introduce Kansas into the Union as a slave state, and Lincoln was delighted to see the Democrats split between supporters of Douglas and supporters of Buchanan.

But some Republicans soon began to treat Douglas as a hero for opposing the president on Kansas. Lincoln wondered why eastern Republicans kept praising Douglas. "Have they concluded that the Republican cause, generally, can be best promoted by sacrificing us here in Illinois?" To Herndon, Lincoln complained that Horace Greeley was "talking up Douglas, an untrue and untried man, a dodger, a wriggler, a tool of the South once and now a snapper at it."

Lincoln did his best to stir the fires of division between the Illinois Democrats. He quietly encouraged Buchanan's Democrats to stand up against Douglas, and he asked some of his powerful supporters to direct Republican funds toward anti-Douglas Democratic newspapers. This, like much else in his early life, would indicate that he did not come to the presidency as the naive, frontier figure populist myth would depict him to be.

In Springfield in June, Lincoln sat in the audience for a Douglas speech in which the Little Giant argued that, after all, popular sovereignty *would* work, since the territories could exclude slavery by refusing to empower police to enforce slavery, and likewise by refusing to enact slave codes. As for the rest, he said, when the Founding Fathers had spoken of equality, they spoke of equality between whites. The Republicans were a bunch of fanatics who had led some Americans to believe that blacks were covered by the Declaration of Independence and were the equals of white men. If they had their way, whites could look forward to the intermarrying of whites and blacks.

At white heat Lincoln began to study the nine Supreme

Court justices' individual Dred Scott decisions to mount an argument against them and Douglas both. In a summer downpour that flooded all the rivers and made transportation difficult even on the Mississippi, the Republicans assembled in the state house in mid-June. In the afternoon a convention nominated Lincoln as "the first and only choice of the Republicans of Illinois for the United States Senate," and in the evening he was to give the speech on which he had worked for the past two weeks, since hearing Douglas.

Among the spittoons of the Hall of Representatives, Lincoln uttered what was to become the formative speech of his generation, and one that served as the template for his future debates with Douglas. It drew on the language of the Constitution, the Declaration of Independence, and the Bible, and though it was full of technical points, its overall message was graspable by people who were not constitutional experts:

"A house divided against itself cannot stand." I believe this government cannot endure, permanently half-*slave* and half-*free*. I do not expect the Union to be *dissolved*—I do not expect the house to *fall*—but I do expect it will cease to be divided. It will become *all* one thing or *all* the other. Either the *opponents* of slavery will arrest the further spread of it, and place it where the public mind shall rest in the belief that it is in course of ultimate extinction; or its advocates will push forward, till it shall become alike lawful in *all* the states, *old* as well as *new*—*north* as well as *south*.

He believed there was a concerted strategy to make the house a house of slavery, with Taney, President Buchanan, *and*

Stephen Douglas its architects. Other less glittering passages of this speech addressed the illogicality of Douglas's position: "That counterfeit logic which concludes that, because I do not want a black woman for a *slave* I must necessarily want her for a *wife*. . . . [I]n some respects she certainly is not my equal; but in her natural right to eat the bread she earns with her own hands she is my equal, and the equal of all others."

According to Herndon the convention was ecstatic over Lincoln's brilliant speech, but some Republicans and Republican newspapers condemned it, especially the reference to the "house divided." "Damn that fool speech; it will be the cause of the death of Lincoln and the republican party," said one commentator. For this speech, which would be an object of the admiration of later generations, was interpreted as threatening an inevitable civil war over slavery. It was out of the widespread public disapproval for what would become one of the famous speeches of the century, and for fear that Lincoln had destroyed his senatorial chances, that on the advice of various Illinois Republicans, he wrote to Douglas challenging him to a series of formal debates "to divide time, and address the same audiences during the present canvas."

Douglas did not need to accept, because his campaign was flourishing, but perhaps he feared how a refusal would be depicted. He agreed to meet in each congressional district except the Second and Sixth, where they had both already spoken. Unlike even his supporters, Lincoln was confident going into the debates that Douglas was inherently dishonest. "Douglas will tell a lie to ten thousand people one day, even though he knows he may have to deny it to five thousand the next." This perception of Douglas sharpened Lincoln's sense of a crusade.

Thus the summer of 1858 turned into one of frenetic activity, in which Lincoln scooted around the state debating Douglas, supported by a far less adequate machine than Douglas had. Senator Douglas moved from debate to debate, speech to speech, in a private railroad car festooned with flags. He enjoyed the company of a secretary, a reporter, a traveling band, and his beautiful wife. Lincoln traveled to some of the debates by oxcart, to others by railroad, to others by stagecoach. Thus the stations of the most famous political dialogue of the century were achieved—Ottawa, Freeport, Galesburg, Quincy, Alton, Jonesboro, and Charleston. Not that Lincoln lacked enthusiasts. For the first debate, at Ottawa on August 21, 1858, a special train seventeen cars long drew Lincoln, as a mere paying passenger, and his supporters into Ottawa, Illinois. A carriage bedecked with evergreens was available to carry him to the wooden platform on Washington Square, where the first Lincoln-Douglas confrontation was to take place.

Douglas proved to be an opportunistic debater. He asked why anyone would question that the Republic could last half slave and half free. Hadn't the Founding Fathers themselves created it that way? Lincoln's doctrines would "cover your prairies with black settlements . . . turn this beautiful state into a free negro colony." Douglas was making a good play to the politics of fear.

Lincoln came back strongly, somehow scenting that the defensive mode was not the one to adopt. Lincoln aligned himself with Henry Clay, who had once said of those who would repress tendencies to liberty and ultimate emancipation "that they must, if they would do this, go back to the era of our Independence, and muzzle the cannon which thunders its annual

THOMAS KENEALLY

joyous return; they must blow out the moral lights around us; they must penetrate the human soul, and eradicate there the love of liberty; and then, and not till then, could they perpetuate slavery in this country!"

Lincoln continued, "We will not have peace upon the question until the opponents of slavery arrest the further spread of it. . . . In the right to eat the bread of his labor without the leave of anyone else, the slave is my equal and the equal of Judge Douglas, and the equal of every living man."

Lincoln's handlers were pleased with the way he took the offensive in this first debate, and told him to continue in that mode. At Freeport, in northwest Illinois, Lincoln arrived holding up a wedge in his hand as a symbol of his hope that his words could drive a wedge into the Democrats. Here, with the threat of rain coming on and fifteen thousand people to address, Lincoln tried to cast attention on the divisions between Buchanan and Douglas: "Can the people of a United States Territory, in any lawful way, against the wish of any citizen of the United States, exclude slavery from its limits prior to the formation of a state constitution?" Buchanan would have said no, Douglas yes. Even with Lincoln's shrill, penetrating voice, even with Douglas's senatorial oratory, one wonders how many of them actually heard the ramified arguments, which would be reproduced in the next day's newspapers.

In the intervening time between debates, Lincoln argued his case at picnics, at crossroad meetings, and even at political rallies marked by balloon ascents. Douglas always fell back on the idea that Lincoln was preaching "Negro citizenship." On the defensive, Lincoln performed poorly at Jonesboro and Charleston, particularly given that Charleston was in southern Illinois, where antiblack attitudes were the strongest. "I am not nor ever have been in favor of making voters or jurors of negroes, nor of qualifying them to hold office, nor to inter-marry with white women." Douglas was thus able to lambaste him with the contrast between what he said in the antislavery north of the state and what he said in the south.

In bad weather the Jonesboro meeting, down near the Kentucky border, attracted an audience of a mere twelve hundred. But in Charleston both sides went to a great deal of trouble. A cavalcade of thirty-two young women representing the states of the Union supported Lincoln. And at Galesburg, where he was on more sympathetic ground, he returned to a frontal attack on the immorality of slavery. "I believe that slavery is wrong, and in a policy springing from that belief that looks to the prevention of the enlargement of that wrong." There were twenty thousand in the crowd, buffeted by a freezing autumn wind, before which Lincoln and Douglas debated. But here as in every town in which they had occurred, the debates were social events, preceded by bands, pageants, marching militia—and those who treated them as a fair could always read the actual text in the next day's paper.

The last of the debates was to be at Alton on the Mississippi in southern Illinois—country that seemed to favor Douglas by being antiabolitionist. Mary herself attended that debate; the Sangamon-Alton railroad ran a half-price excursion train from Springfield, and both the Lincolns and their son Robert, then a fifteen-year-old schoolboy wearing the uniform of the Springfield cadets, were aboard.

The weather was nearly as severe as that on the day of the Galesburg debate, and on arrival Mary was further depressed to see the streets decked out with Democratic Party slogans, and processions of Democrats carrying banners bearing such slogans as POPULAR SOVEREIGNTY. Abe was lucky to find a Republican, whom he sent over to where Mary stood to reassure her that though the Democrats were rowdy, there were loyal Republican souls among the crowd.

Lincoln blazed at Alton. In a memorable stanza of his speech, he equated slavery with the divine right of kings—the latter an odious principle in the United States. "No matter in what shape it comes, whether from the mouth of a king who seeks to bestride the people of his own nation and live by the fruit of their labor, or from one race of men as an apology for enslaving another race, it is the same tyrannical principle."

Lincoln had become more optimistic as the debates went on. He went into the elections knowing he had made sixty speeches, traveled more than 4,300 miles around the state, and with other Republicans brought in 125,000 votes for Republican state candidates as against 121,000 cast for Douglas Democrats. But the Republican votes were not evenly spread, and on a seat-by-seat basis, Democrat candidates won 46 to the Republicans' 41. When the legislature convened in Springfield in January, the vote was along party lines, even Buchanan Democrats voting for Douglas. Lincoln spoke of the "emotions of defeat" settling upon his household. In the pause after frenetic electioneering, the "hypo" was upon him and upon Mary Todd too. On top of everything they had sacrificed a great deal of income to the fight against Douglas.

Lincoln, however, had a sense of the notable nature of the debates, and wrote to a Chicago newspaper editor of his acquaintance, asking that a full set of the debates be sent by express. He saw his contests with Douglas as the high point of his life, and believed that the physical record of them might comfort him in the obscurity that lay ahead. He knew that the Douglas worldview, and even more so the Buchanan one, was doomed, but he saw his role in its future destruction as that of a mere political foot soldier.

As late as February 1859, a client saw that Lincoln was still depressed and commiserated with him. Lincoln explained that he felt like "the boy who stumped [*sic*] his toe. I am too big to cry and too badly hurt to laugh."

Meanwhile, to console herself, Mary had taken to shopping. At her brother-in-law Clark Smith's store, she bought six yards of plaid silk, ten and a half yards of cambric and cashmere, and various ruches, chenille, buttons, and stockings. She did not make her own clothing, however, but turned over her purchases to the Irish dressmaker Madame La Barth, whose French *nom de couture* saved her from the stigma Mary customarily placed upon the Irish. Fortunately Abe suddenly received a contested fee of $4,800 from the Illinois Central Railway.

To his surprise he was forced to go on combining his legal tasks with political appearances, for his debates with Douglas had, despite his failure to reach the Senate, brought him a measure of national renown. A few Illinois papers began mentioning Lincoln as a possible 1860 presidential nominee. A friend took him for a walk after court in Bloomingdale and told him that in the East, Republicans were asking about this Lincoln who had given Douglas such a run. Lincoln told an Illinois editor who wanted to announce his candidacy that "I do not think myself fit for the presidency." One reason was that he did not consider that he had adequate administrative ability, and the idea of the patronage involved in the presidency, the numerous political favors that would need to be repaid to clamorous party interests, daunted him. Whether utterly sincere or not, he advised one Republican willing to promote his candidacy, "I really think it best for our cause that no concerted effort, such as you suggest, should be made."

He took time to advise Salmon P. Chase, a Republican antislavery man eminent in Ohio, that he thought that "the introduction of a proposition for repeal of the Fugitive Slave Law, into the next Republican National Convention, will explode the Convention and the party." That is, slaveholders' right to retrieve their escaped property should be maintained, because the political consequences of any other option would be disastrous. His power to advise someone as eminent as the godly, ambitious Chase—one of the chief contenders to become the Republican candidate for the presidency—showed that his fear of being reduced to the role of humble party hack had been obliterated by his eloquence in the Douglas debates.

He embraced the chance to speak on other issues, such as the invention of steam plows, his enthusiasm for such inventions all the greater because they brought the subsistence farmer into the cash economy, into the milieu of self-improvement, into the possibility of literacy and numeracy. At the Wisconsin State Agricultural Society in Milwaukee, he attacked the idea that "all laborers are necessarily either *hired* laborers or *slaves,*" a favorite Douglas proposition. "There is no such thing as a freeman being fatally fixed for life in the condition of a hired laborer." Again, his own success, and indeed his own self-effacement, conditioned him to see all men as ascendant in society, liberated by

American Republican classlessness. Men were not stuck at the "mud-sill" level of society. "The speaker himself had been a hired man twenty-eight years ago," Lincoln told an Indianapolis crowd. "He didn't think he was worse off than a slave. He might not be doing as much good as he could, but he was now working for himself."

In the autumn and winter of 1859–60, though Lincoln was increasingly cited as a potential presidential candidate, other far more eminent and accomplished Republicans were considered better presidential material. The most eminent was William Henry Seward, a former senator and governor of New York. Salmon P. Chase, the devoutly religious lawyer from Ohio, was also considered a favorite for the nomination. There were former Whigs, such as Justice John McLean and Edward Bates, who stood higher than Lincoln in the party nationally. And it was quite a prize in prospect, that nomination. Whoever received it had a good chance, purely because of the split between the Douglas Democrats and those who more radically supported the South.

Lincoln was back working on the circuit, unleashing the bolts of his oratory in country courthouses, when the story reached the press of John Brown's attempt to capture Harpers Ferry, Virginia, with its Federal arsenal, and incite a slave rebellion. Lincoln was appalled by the fact that Democrats blamed the Brown uprising on Republican fervor, and on his own antislavery sentiments. But even while he went around the circuit, important men in Springfield and Chicago were forming a coalition in his support.

In January 1860 Lincoln's "peculiar friends" met with him in

Springfield and began to plan his nomination. They included Logan, Judge Davis, Lamon, Herndon, Swett, and a Chicago newspaperman named Norman Judd—all men who shared Lincoln's Whiggish ideas about American improvements. Sickened by President Buchanan's attempt to admit Kansas as a slave state, they knew also that Lincoln was a sensible fellow who thought abolitionism dangerous, and freed slaves likely to reduce the wages of white laborers. Moreover, they wanted for Illinois and its right-thinking men increased authority and the paid places, posts, and honors of which the presidency was a fount.

8

LINCOLN WENT TO New York City that bitter and fraught winter, answering an invitation to speak at Henry Ward Beecher's Plymouth Church in Brooklyn. Many leading New York Republicans were opposed to Seward's candidacy, not least because he had at one time promoted an alliance between the Republicans and Stephen Douglas. To some extent Lincoln's appearance was designed to test his palatability for New York and New England Republican tastes. Because of demand, his speech had been moved to Cooper Union, where it was to be part of a series by eminent western Republicans. When Lincoln arrived in New York by train and was met by leading Republicans of the anti-Seward variety, it must have become apparent to him that, should he perform well, Horace Greeley of the *Tribune*, perhaps the most important Republican organ in the country, was willing to throw support his way.

Abraham was accommodated at the Astor House, the city's premier hotel, and on the day of his speech in February, he went to Mathew Brady's studio and had a photograph taken for potential distribution throughout the Northeast. Like the few earlier photographs that survive, it shows a lean, clean-shaven, tall man, somewhere between august and rough hewn, possessing an appearance of tentative strength but already bearing an unreachable, unquenchable sorrow in his profound eyes. He seems a creature hewn from barely violated forests, and polished and grooved by the flow of primeval streams. People who would hate him for his success in the election of 1860 actually called him King Log, as if he were a shaft that had been floated down the Sangamon to the Illinois and to the Mississippi and out its mouth, washing ashore by implacable accident on the more sullied banks of the Potomac.

The day of the Cooper Union speech was bitter, and the wind mounted and snow fell as night came on. Nonetheless fifteen hundred Republicans made their way through the blizzard to hear Lincoln speak. Some of them, it seemed, looked at the lecturer and wondered if they had made the right choice, for a witness said that there was "something weird, rough, and uncultivated" about Abraham Lincoln. Introduced by William Cullen Bryant, the Republican power broker, poet, and newspaper editor, Lincoln began hesitantly, and his high-pitched western twang raised further doubts in the minds of urbane New Yorkers. But his power as a speaker was his sense of mission—his fury to prove among other things that the Founding Fathers had frequently voted to let Congress regulate slavery and saw it as a practice to be limited, not licensed as a right. He quoted Thomas Jefferson: "It is still in our power to direct the process of emancipation, and deportation, peaceably, and in such slow degrees, as if the evil will wear off insensibly; and their places be, *pari passu*, filled up by free white laborers."

No one before Roger Taney and Stephen Douglas, Lincoln told the crowd, ever questioned the authority of the Federal government to control slavery in Federal territories. The South wants "us to stop calling slavery wrong and join them, in acts as well as words, in calling slavery *right*. Only when the whole atmosphere is 'disinfected from all taint of opposition to slavery' will they quit blaming us for their troubles. . . . If slavery is right, then all laws and all state constitutions against it must be swept away."

In his report a young journalist from the *Tribune,* Noah Brooks, an extensive commentator on the age in which he lived, and a man devoted to Lincoln from that night, recorded the increasing enthusiasm and the gales of applause that interrupted Lincoln's speech. Brooks quoted a member of the audience who said of Lincoln, "He's the greatest man since St. Paul." And, bent on its task of exalting Lincoln and disparaging Seward, the *Tribune* reported that "no man ever before made such an impression on his first appeal to a New-York audience." Quite apart from any political convenience sought by Horace Greeley and others, it had been a triumph.

After his New York success, he spoke at Providence, Rhode Island, and in New Hampshire, where Phillips Exeter, the preparatory school at which Robert was being groomed for Harvard, was located. Such was the contrast between Lincoln's print-deprived and rail-splitting adolescence and that of his favored sons! But Robert never seemed to evince much gratitude for the contrast (Herndon said that he was very much Mary Todd's sullen child). One Sunday Lincoln consented to go to church with Robert, and then shared dinner with him before they went back to Robert's rooms, where one of the boy's housemates entertained Abraham Lincoln with a banjo. In Hartford he met white-bearded Gideon Welles, a powerful Connecticut Republican and newspaperman, whose positive remarks in private conversation helped convince Lincoln that he might after all have a chance for the presidential nomination.

. . .

When the Illinois Republican convention met in Decatur in May 1860, in a huge tent or wigwam structure specially erected for the occasion, Lincoln's cousin John Hanks and a friend of Hanks's marched down the aisle carrying a banner fixed between two fence rails: ABRAHAM LINCOLN, THE RAIL CANDIDATE FOR PRESIDENT, read the banner. TWO RAILS FROM A LOT OF 3,000 MADE IN 1830 BY THOS. HANKS AND ABE LINCOLN—WHOSE FATHER WAS THE FIRST PIONEER OF MACON COUNTY.

The convention went wild, and the only figure who was not delighted at such a vote-winning display was Abraham himself. There were the split rails, putatively cut by him in his era of slavery. Two from a lot of three thousand—the fruit of intense rustic labor, the symbol of numb endurance and of a past he would rather put aside. But the idea of "Abe" the rail splitter was released into the air and was hungrily taken up by the American public. Of course he was nominated by the Illinois delegates.

A headquarters was eventually set up in the Fremont Hotel in Chicago, as the base for the promotion of Lincoln's candidacy. The hotel was five blocks from where the Republican convention would ultimately take place, the Chicago Wig-Wam. From the Fremont and within its rooms, the Lincoln team began to lobby delegates. They noticed that there was a great deal of goodwill toward Lincoln, for he had not had such a visible career as to have collected enemies. Orville Browning and Herndon did not think he could possibly win, however, and their support for his candidacy would drop off.

The national delegates assembled in Chicago in mid-May. Neither Lincoln nor Mary attended—it was not customary for candidates to do so. In Springfield, Mary awaited news at home, and Abraham lingered in his office.

Early messages he received from Judd had declared "nothing will beat us but old fogy politicians," and, "I tell you that your chances are not the worst . . . be not too expectant, but rely upon our discretion. Again I say brace your nerves for any result." Lincoln himself had already sent off a message to Davis: "Make no contracts that will bind me." On the first ballot Seward scored 173.5 delegates, Lincoln 102. When he received the telegram announcing these figures, a bigger vote than he had expected, he could not stay in his office any longer but went to the *Sangamo Journal* office. A further telegram arrived: The second ballot had seen Seward pick up only 11 delegates, but Lincoln 79. Some witnesses say that Lincoln had gone off to a local court for a game of handball when the final telegram arrived. It had an electrifying effect: TO LINCOLN YOU ARE NOMINATED.

On the floor of the Chicago convention, when in the final count four Ohio votes moved from Chase to Lincoln to make his nomination possible, there was an uproar, said a witness, like "all the hogs ever slaughtered in Cincinnati giving their death squeals together." The convention selected for him as running mate Hannibal Hamlin, former Democrat from Maine.

On receipt of the news, Lincoln told the supporters gathered in the *Journal* office, "Well, gentlemen, there is a little woman at our house who is probably more interested in this dispatch than I am; if you will excuse me, I will take the dispatch up and let her see it." As the town rocked with band music, with serenaders and congratulatory processions, Lincoln was besieged for some days in his home. Enthusiastic crowds surrounded the white frame residence, and when Lincoln told them that he would like to have them all indoors if only the place were big enough, a spectator shouted, "We will give you a larger house on the Fourth of next March" (the date of inauguration at that time). Lincoln was fiendishly busy with his correspondence, and with receiving leading Republicans, including possible claimants for cabinet positions, such as Seward and Salmon P. Chase. Mexican diplomats, encouraged by his opposition to the war of 1846, came to express their hope for a co-operative relationship between the two republics. So that he could deal with the crowds of place hunters, journalists, and others, he was offered the use of the governor's room in the state house, where, free from interruption by playful Tad, he received visitors and worked on his enormous correspondence. He needed to forestall misstatements, particularly regarding the myths about his childhood, likely to appear in the fifteen campaign biographies that would be issued that summer. And even though these were written by Republicans, as they mythologized his childhood and took all the genuine bitterness out, they seemed to be subscribing to the Jeffersonian myth that nothing dishonest, cunning, or dishonorable could come out of a log cabin. This concept caused Lincoln dark and edgy amusement.

Lincoln had also to assure one correspondent that he had never been a member of any Know-Nothing lodge. He needed to correct the proofs of his famous New York speech, and to console by letter a friend of Robert's who had failed to gain entry to Harvard (Robert had been accepted). And to reply to eleven-year-old Grace Beddell, who wrote suggesting that he grow whiskers: ". . . you would look a great deal better for your face is so thin." "Having never worn any," Lincoln responded, "do you not think people would call it a piece of silly affection if I were to begin it now?" Many, including himself, were becoming concerned about matters of style and clothing. He was reconsidering his wardrobe, and a group of New York Republicans sent him a quite serious memorial stating that their "candid determination" was that his appearance of gauntness would be less obvious if he cultivated whiskers and wore standing collars to hide his scrawny neck. Later in the year he would yield to Miss Beddell's and his fellow Republicans' advice and begin to grow a beard.

To deal with the mass of work, he employed a secretary, a young German American named John Nicolay, who had previously worked as a secretary-cum-archivist in the state attorney general's office. Nicolay would be Lincoln's familiar from that point on. Occasionally the armies of people seeking Federal posts, large and small, brought him a sense of his inadequacy for the presidency, and an awareness of the contingent factors by which he had become the Republican candidate. He believed he had been "accidentally selected."

The Democratic convention in Charleston had split between those such as Jefferson Davis, favoring a prescriptive Federal slave code for the territories, and the supporters of Douglas and the earnestly held principle of popular sovereignty. Douglas could not get the two-thirds support he needed for nomination. The stalemated party, including many Southern "bolters," came to a new convention in Baltimore, but the "bolters" walked out again and held their own convention, nominating their own candidate, John C. Breckinridge, President Buchanan's vice president. On June 18 the main Baltimore convention nominated Douglas. The Democratic schism was now a matter of fact. Lin-

coln seemed destined to win because of the division of the Democratic vote between Douglas, the Southern Democrat candidate Breckinridge, and the residual Whig-Know-Nothing
candidate, John Bell.

In the meantime Southern Democrats and their Northern
friends, in editorials and public meetings, declared that if Lincoln was elected, hundreds of thousands of fugitive slaves would
"emigrate to their friends" in the North, "and be placed by them
side by side in competition with white men." This was the message of the Little Giant, Stephen A. Douglas, who began almost
at once to conduct his own nationwide campaign. It was un-
precedented then for a candidate to do his own campaigning,
but he felt that the issue was so great that he must do so—to run
as a true *national,* not sectional, candidate, and to promise to
save the Union. The demands of the campaign would help has-
ten his death, which would occur as the bloody casualties began
to mount in late 1861.

A courageous Douglas, fearing that the split in Democratic
ranks would leave Lincoln the presidency, went South to warn
people about the dangers of rhetoric concerning secession. Southern Democrats, however, saw Douglas as almost as vicious as
Lincoln.

Lincoln himself aroused in the South a fever of revulsion
and hysteria. According to the accepted rhetoric, he was a supporter of slave uprisings. The election of Lincoln, went the fer-
vid message, would unleash mayhem, miscegenation, and the
end of freedom, and would be adequate grounds for secession
from the Union. Billy Herndon supplied Lincoln and Nicolay in
their office at the state house with the latest editions of rabid
Southern newspapers. Lincoln was depicted as a horrid-looking

wretch, a bloodthirsty tyrant, a chimpanzee, a promoter of slave uprising indistinguishable in attitude from John Brown. Unionists in the South warned the Republican Party that hysteria and madness ruled the hour, and that Lincoln was being demonized as a grotesque gargoyle, a walking *casus belli*. "What is it that I could say that would quiet alarm?" asked a bewildered Lincoln of those who would have him make yet another appeasing statement to the South. "Is it that no interference by the government, with slaves or slavery within the states, is intended? I have said this so often already, that a repetition of it is but mockery, bearing the appearance of weakness." Indeed, he was right. The South was far gone in its pathology.

His unwillingness to make too many statements might have been due to such wise advice as that of William Cullen Bryant, the editor who had introduced his famous Cooper Union speech. Bryant advised him early "to make no speeches, write no letters as a candidate." His record spoke for itself, and new notations on it might cast up nuances that could be twisted by the press, North and South, into great campaign issues.

During Lincoln's silence, journalists began to notice how political Mary Todd Lincoln was by comparison with other politicians' wives. Talkative and well informed, she made good newspaper copy, especially since Lincoln had closed down and referred people to his previous statements. Like some presidents' wives since, Mary would later discover the perils of being an outspoken first lady.

Lincoln had the sagacity early in his campaign to avoid any alliances, either with the Seward-style easterners, with the more abolitionist Salmon P. Chase, with Charles Sumner, another abolitionist leader in the Senate, or with any other faction. At the lowest estimation this meant that he would distribute posts according to his own wisdom, and the result would be that he did not exalt any Republican group over another. At best it was the high wisdom that acknowledged that he needed all factions to elect him. It was a principle he would reiterate over and over again to party notables at his dinner table at Eighth and Jackson that summer.

Precious, precocious, early-reading Willie Lincoln had in the meantime caught a form of scarlet fever, and it intensified his parents' secretly harbored concerns about loss and defeat. Mary wrote, "I scarcely know, how I would bear up, under defeat. I trust we will not have the trial." The family was caught between the rankest abuse from Southern commentators and condemnation by the fathers of abolition, Garrison and Wendell Phillips, who considered Lincoln's brand of gradualism immoral and cowardly.

In 1860 not all states' elections occurred on the same day, and those that were held in Pennsylvania and Indiana in October served as indicators for Republicans' hopes. Republican governors and legislatures were elected in both states, and Lincoln wrote to Seward, "It now really looks as if the Government is about to fall into our hands." He spent election day, November 6, in his office in Springfield, emerging at about three o'clock to cross the square and vote. Then, with a number of supporters, he went off to the telegraph office to which the popular returns from around the country would be wired. Lincoln disposed himself crookedly on the telegraph office sofa as the news came in. Illinois had gone strongly his way, it became apparent. So had New England. Figures from the upper and lower North looked promising, and New York hung in the balance, but by midnight the returns from New York appeared to be conclusive.

Huge crowds had gathered in the square in front of the statehouse, and Lincoln supporters ran from the telegraph office to acquaint them with the returns. Lincoln was taken over to the statehouse to a celebration dinner, through crowds of supporters singing, "Ain't you glad you joined the Republicans, down in Illinois!" The dinner had been arranged by Mary and other Republican women, who crowded around jubilantly calling Lincoln "Mr. President."

By 1:30 A.M. the less complimentary returns from the South were coming in. Lincoln sent Mary home ahead, and went back to the telegraph office, walking home at last aware that although he would win the North, he did not have an absolute majority. He hoped he might garner, however, an absolute majority of the electoral college, and thus have strong legitimacy as president. In those streets, walking away from the riotous joy of Republican supporters, which would occupy the center of town all night, he felt the dead weight of the office he so dearly desired.

He would never for another breathing moment escape it. "Well, boys," he would tell journalists the next day, "your troubles are over now, mine have just begun."

The final tally of electoral votes for Lincoln would be 180. Breckenridge, who carried most of the South, received 72; there were 39 for Bell, who won Virginia, Kentucky, and Tennessee; and despite his 1.3 million votes, ultimately only 12 for Douglas, given that he had won only two states, Missouri and New Jersey. The previous imbalance between Lincoln's star and Douglas's had now been savagely adjusted. The tide had run out beneath the Little Giant.

9

EVEN BEFORE all the votes were in, the South Carolina governor had called the legislature into special session to authorize a state convention on the dissolution of the Union and the formation of a Southern Confederacy. Henry Raymond, the editor of the *New York Times,* pleaded with Lincoln to issue a statement clarifying his intentions. Lincoln stood firm. He did not want any words he uttered to add to the conflagration. He feared that anything he said now, instead of calming the waters, would be held up by "the *Washington Constitution* [a pro-Southern Washington, D.C., daily] and its class . . . as an open declaration of war against them [the South]."

A number of friends of his, in a state of stress about the forthcoming secession convention in South Carolina, urged him to allow popular sovereignty-based extension of slavery into territories south of the old Missouri Compromise line. Outraged, he answered, "I am sorry any Republican inclines to dally with Pop. Sov. of any sort. It acknowledges that slavery has equal rights with liberty, and surrenders all we have contended for."

The South Carolina secession convention came together and decided on December 20 to pass an ordinance of secession and to send commissioners to every slaveholding state to invite them to join "a great slaveholding Confederacy." In the intervening period, while Buchanan still held power, Mississippi followed South Carolina, and then, on January 10, so did Florida. Alabama, Georgia, Louisiana, and Texas joined the seceding states by February 1. On February 4 in Montgomery, Alabama, commissioners from all the seceding states met to bring the Confederacy into being. Through all this, when many in his ranks panicked, Lincoln remained silent except in some private letters, one of them to the great Georgian statesman and future Confederate vice president, Alexander Stephens, in which he defined his position. It was that the South would not be in any greater danger of losing its slaves under him than it had been in the days of Washington. "I suppose, however, this does not meet the case. You think slavery is *right* and ought to be extended; while we think it is *wrong* and ought to be restricted. That is, I suppose, the rub."

Throughout the secession period, Lincoln mistakenly believed that, according to the principle of necessity, the South would not secede when it came to the point. For it was not in the interests of the Southern states to become an embattled slave union cut off from the North. Many of the slaveholding states seemed to realize this, for as the Lincoln family leased out their house and packed up to leave Springfield, although many Southern states had gone through the motions of secession, Maryland, Kentucky, Delaware, Missouri, Virginia, Arkansas, and North Carolina were still in the Union. Lincoln told Herndon that "he could not in his heart believe that the South designed the overthrow of the Government." This belief may have been the greatest misjudgment of his political life.

In December 1860, while still in Springfield, Lincoln had started choosing his cabinet. Seward, "a slouching, slender figure; a head like a wise macaw's," was to be secretary of state.

Salmon P. Chase, the Republican Party's chief ideologue, who had his eye on the 1864 election, became secretary of the treasury. Edward Bates, a squat Missourian in his late sixties who still considered himself a Whig, was invited to be attorney general. The fact that he came from a border slave state added to his attraction as a potential cabinet member. Gideon Welles, the former Democrat and latter-day Republican from Connecticut, who had encouraged Lincoln, was appointed secretary of the navy. A less reputable figure, Simon Cameron, a tall Pennsylvania businessman of questionable probity, had such party influence that he sought the treasury post for himself, but after much argument and with some distaste, Lincoln made him secretary of war. Lincoln said of Cameron that his "very name stinks in the nostrils of the people for his corruption," and was reluctant to appoint him. The other promised cabinet post, secretary of the interior, went to Caleb Smith of Indiana.

Through this period of cabinet building and interest squaring, the garrison of three Union forts in Charleston Harbor was consolidated into one, Fort Sumter. Lincoln feared that Buchanan would surrender Sumter and, if this shameful course was taken, Lincoln intended to make a public statement that he would ensure the fort was retaken after his inauguration in March.

Even Lincoln's future secretary of state, Seward, came up with a plan to buy off the South by admitting New Mexico as a slave state. Seward was also active in a Peace Convention, which met in Washington on February 4. He and other Northerners were busy with stratagems to thwart or delay the obvious manifestations of secession. Most of the gestures they wanted to make, however, involved extending slavery, and—as Lincoln put it—trying to buy for the administration the right, already earned, to take power in

March. Despite his belief that ultimately the South wouldn't secede, Lincoln kept a clear determination and a cool head, and dealt with the private manifestations of his depressive nature, the disabling dread that could creep up on him and destroy his rest.

On the final afternoon in Springfield, Lincoln organized a few last things at his office, ran over the books, and gave Billy Herndon instructions for the completion of unsettled and unfinished matters. He then crossed the room and threw himself on the office sofa, "which, after many years of service, had been moved against the wall for support." He asked Herndon to let the Lincoln and Herndon sign go on hanging downstairs. "If I live, I'm coming back sometime, and then we'll go right on practicing law as if nothing had ever happened." A little earlier he had been to Coles County to visit his stepmother, Sally. By the farmhouse fire, with the wind blowing at the windows, he held her hand. Some said he ordered a stone placed over Tom Lincoln's grave, but credible others dispute it. But the distance between Springfield and Washington, between state legislator and circuit lawyer on the one hand, and chief magistracy and the White House on the other, was such as to make a man settle his affairs, just in case.

Having rented out their home, the Lincolns had spent their last days in Springfield in the Chenery House hotel. Although it was hard to believe in exultant and apparently cordial Springfield, there were many threats abroad against Lincoln. Aware of this, he wanted Mary to travel separately from him. Since Mary had her own strong opinions on this, the best Lincoln could do was to arrange that he and Robert would leave by one train, and that Mary, Willie, and Tad would meet them in Indianapolis by a later one.

So Lincoln and Robert and their entourage went off to the depot at the Great Western Railroad, where, that icy day, a thousand people had gathered, demanding a speech. "To this place, and the kindness of these people, I owe everything," Abraham said. "Here my children have been born, and one is buried. I now leave, not knowing when or whether ever I may return, with a task before me greater than ever rested upon Washington." Then, since such a reference was necessary, he invoked the Divine Being, earnestly but in a somehow unspecific manner.

His traveling companions included John Nicolay and a more recently hired and adoring twenty-three-year-old secretary named John Hay. Besides the secretaries and Robert, Ward Lamon, heavily armed, also accompanied the president-elect, and Elmer Ellsworth, a young militiaman–law clerk for whom the Lincolns had a special affection. Orville Browning and Gov. Richard Yates intended to go as far as Indianapolis. Lincoln's military escort consisted of officers who would have a large future in the coming conflict—Maj. David Hunter, Col. Edwin Sumner, Capt. John Pope.

At Indianapolis, Lincoln made a firm speech, asking, "If the United States should merely hold and retake its own forts and other property, and collect the duties on foreign importations, or even withhold the mails from places where they were habitually violated—would any or all of these things be 'invasion' or 'coercion'?" For forts in the South *had* been occupied by Rebels, and post offices, treasuries, and customs houses taken over by secessionist states. Yet he still believed secession to be a mere foolish phase, a show of rebelliousness.

After Indianapolis he went through Columbus, then addressed the German Americans of Cincinnati. People remarked on how he "threw off his overcoat in an offhand, easy manner," in a backwoods style that caused many good-natured remarks. But he was not at ease. At one stop he snapped at Robert in a hotel room when a draft of his inaugural address was temporarily misplaced. He had been working on it since Springfield and believed it might yet, with its sane, level tone, save the Union. Rolling into upstate New York, he heard that Jefferson Davis had taken an oath as president of the Confederacy, and the news, by giving a new solidity to the Confederacy, shook him so much that he apologized to the crowd at the statehouse at Albany for having neither the voice nor the strength for a longer address. In New York City, traveling in a barouche to the Astor House hotel, he saw banners pleading, WELCOME ABRAHAM LINCOLN. WE BEG FOR COMPROMISE. Walt Whitman, seated in a traffic-stalled omnibus, saw the president-elect pass through the reticent crowd and surmised that "many an assassin's knife and pistol lurked in hip or breast-pocket there." At City Hall, in reply to a welcome from the Democratic mayor, Fernando Wood, who called for "fraternal relations between the States," he thanked New Yorkers for their kind reception, acknowledging that they "do not by a large majority agree with me."

A hostile press ridiculed him for his pronunciation of the word "inauguration," and for hanging his large hands over the edge of his box at the opera and wearing black kid gloves. Nonetheless he had met with many of the city's financial leaders and had crucially impressed them.

Heading for Washington, he addressed the assembly and senate of New Jersey. In Philadelphia, where he faced a number of engagements, Lincoln had a meeting with Alan Pinkerton, the Scottish-born secret agent for the Philadelphia, Wilmington &

Baltimore Railroad (later founder of the eponymous detective agency). Pinkerton told Lincoln that his detectives had uncovered a plot to murder him in Baltimore, where travelers to Washington changed trains. Baltimore was the chief city of Maryland, a border slave state, and was full of pro-Southern sentiment. Pinkerton suggested that Lincoln should go through Baltimore earlier than planned, but Lincoln refused to give up his engagements for the next day in Philadelphia and Harrisburg. Meanwhile, Gen. Winfield Scott also reported from Washington that his agents had uncovered the plot to kill the president-elect in Baltimore, and that Lincoln must at all costs avoid the city.

Scheduled to leave for Philadelphia, Baltimore, and Washington the morning after his Harrisburg event, instead he left the town late that night on a special train. In case there were watchers, the telegraph lines were cut as he pulled out of the Harrisburg depot. At Philadelphia he donned a disguise, and a carriage took him to the Baltimore line. There Lincoln was ushered aboard a sleeping car that took him as far as Baltimore, where a fresh engine took over his car and drew it on to Washington. Lincoln, in "a brown Kossuth hat" and an overcoat (and accompanied by the heavily armed Lamon), arrived in the nation's capital at 6:30 A.M. He had traveled separately from Mary, who would arrive by special train at the appropriate hour. Mary and their sons arrived safely, although their train had been intercepted in Baltimore by a pro-Southern mob that yelled insults about the "black ape."

A story got around that he had crept into Washington disguised as a highlander, or even as a woman. Much derided for sneaking into Washington, he pledged never to be persuaded to skulk again. But even here at the nation's heart he was not safe, since the city, across the river from Virginia, lived in daily terror—or, in some cases, hope—of a Southern invasion.

Lincoln went first to Willard's, the famous and splendid hotel near the White House. Even that early, the city seemed a more frenetic place than he had remembered. Everything looked even more incomplete. The beams of the Capitol's building apparatus sat on its skeletal dome like a confession of naked unreadiness. Similarly the Treasury, near Willard's, was unfinished, and the Washington Monument, like the Republic itself, was a white unfinished shaft in the distance.

Tussles were already under way within the proposed cabinet. Seward tendered his resignation on Montgomery Blair's appointment as postmaster general. Seward had a long-running grievance against Frank Blair, Sr., the leader of the powerful Blair clan of Missouri. And the bruised egos from the Republican convention had not yet been assuaged. Meanwhile, in the last days of his catastrophic administration, James Buchanan refused to surrender Fort Sumter to the forces of South Carolina.

It proved a harsh welcome for Mary. Many Tidewater aristocrats were still in town—Virginia had not yet seceded—and unaware of the Kentucky-Illinois class system, they lumped her and her husband together as boorish. To be a Todd of Kentucky meant nothing to the hubristic Virginians.

Lincoln was not hurt at all. He was used to being discounted—except as an orator. He paid enormous attention to what he would have to say on March 4, the day of the inauguration. It proved to be a characteristic late-winter day, steely and overcast. General Scott had stationed troops along Pennsylvania Avenue and around the Capitol with the specific instructions, for the first time in American history, to protect the incoming president's life. Near the east portico of the Capitol, a rostrum had been built, with barriers to separate the inauguration party from the public, again for the first time in history. The old republican piety of the president's being merely the first among citizens had come under threat of the assassin's bullet, a threat that would never leave the American political scene.

This day above all validated Mary Todd Lincoln's decision to marry Abraham. No security considerations could keep her separate from him, and she beamed as, after he was sworn in by Chief Justice Taney, Lincoln gave his inaugural address. In the face of secessionist frenzy, the president made as conciliatory a speech as anyone could have, or at least anyone who believed that the restriction, and not the extension, of slavery was a founding principle of the Union. "Apprehension seems to exist among the people of the Southern States that by the accession of a Republican administration, their property, and their peace, and personal security are to be endangered. There has never been any reasonable cause for such apprehension." He quoted his former speeches: "I have no purpose, directly or indirectly, to interfere with the institution of slavery in the states where it exists. I believe I have no lawful right to do so."

He quoted the constitutional guarantee that no person who was a slave in one state could achieve freedom by escaping into another. "All members of Congress swear their support to the whole Constitution—to this provision as much as to any other." He acknowledged that unlike previous presidents he entered his brief constitutional term of four years "under great and peculiar difficulty." He argued that for one state to break the compact of the United States, all would need to rescind it lawfully.

"I therefore consider that in view of the Constitution and the laws, the Union is unbroken; and to the extent of my ability I shall take care, as the Constitution itself expressly enjoins upon me, that the laws of the Union be faithfully executed in all the States." The mails, "unless repelled," would continue to go to all parts of the Union. He warned of the "so desperate a step" involved in secession. "If the minority will not acquiesce," however, "the majority must, or the government must cease." For if any state could secede when it liked, what was to prevent a minority of Rebel states from themselves further seceding from the proposed Confederacy? The Confederacy would itself resist such secession, just as the Union resisted secession now. In fact,

> Physically speaking, we cannot separate. We cannot remove our respective sections from each other, nor build an impassable wall between them. A husband and wife may be divorced, and go out of the presence, and beyond the reach of each other; but the different parts of our country cannot do this. They cannot but remain face to face; and intercourse, either amicable or hostile, must continue between them.

In the meantime he affirmed that the only way to change the Constitution and its guarantee of property in slaves was by the will of the people:

> In *your* hands, my dissatisfied fellow countrymen, and not in *mine,* is the momentous issue of civil war. The government will not assail *you.* You can have no conflict, without being yourselves the aggressors. *You* have no oath registered in heaven to destroy the government, while *I* shall have the most solemn one to "preserve, protect and defend" it.

10

THAT NIGHT, surrounded by many Todd sisters and cousins, Mary, in watered blue silk, was the queen of the inaugural ball at a temporary structure behind City Hall. She danced with Stephen Douglas.

Lincoln knew that Maj. Robert Anderson's troops in Fort Sumter needed either to be resupplied or to surrender. So he had to leave the ball early, to attend to this first great problem of the new civil conflict. In the small hours of the following morning, at Lincoln's office—"the shop"—at the White House, at the oak table used by previous chief executives, elderly and crotchety Gen. Winfield Scott advised the president that forcing the relief of Fort Sumter would require a third of the present standing army. Lincoln must consult his cabinet and high-ranking officers.

More of an appeaser, Seward was for evacuating the fort. Montgomery Blair advised Lincoln to hang on to it, and Gideon Welles, secretary of the navy, had already stated that, though Sumter was difficult, the equally endangered Fort Pickens in Florida could be reinforced and held. But Sumter remained the test case. Stirring the pot were the radical Republicans, led by Senator Sumner, who condemned Lincoln for coming from the "old fogey" wing of the Whig Party and being hesitant.

Lincoln, oppressed by the potentialities of the season, the great risk of war, decided not to act until Sumter's supplies ran out, rather than himself precipitate a civil war. So he devoted himself to diplomatic appointments, and to office seekers who came to him in increasing numbers. He felt "like a man letting lodgings at one end of his house, while the other end was on fire."

Seward would chide him in a memorandum toward the end of the first month of his presidency that the administration was "without a policy, either foreign or domestic." It was true enough, except for the fact that the ground kept shifting beneath the government's feet. He had already rejected General Scott's concept that he should abandon Sumter as a concession. "He could not, consistently with his conviction of his duty, and with the policy he had enunciated in his Inaugural, order the evacuation of Sumter." About the time of Seward's complaint, Lincoln gave his cabinet his final direction on the matter of Sumter. He would send a supply and reinforcement fleet to Charleston Harbor to relieve the fort, and if the Rebels began firing, the choice would be upon their heads, not on the administration's. Secretary of the Navy Welles applauded this policy, but Seward caused confusion by taking it upon himself to separate the re-supply convoy from the military one. His motives were that he had already promised the South Carolinians, unilaterally, and in an attempt to stop them from attacking Sumter, that the fort would be evacuated. It was not within his portfolio to do so, but because he was such a notable Republican, they tended to believe that Seward's promise was identical with the promise of that western clodhopper, Lincoln. Seward had clouded the waters considerably and given the South Carolinians grounds for feeling misled when Lincoln took a different line.

On April 6 Lincoln sent a message to the governor of South Carolina about the column of supply ships that was approaching Sumter. They would not open fire on any shore installations, he guaranteed. On April 12, with the resupply ships off Charleston Harbor, the artillery of South Carolina, the Palmetto State, opened fire on Sumter. On the thirteenth, the Palmettos permitted the withdrawal of Anderson and his men by the Union ships.

The firing on the Federal flag at Fort Sumter galvanized not only Republicans but many Democrats—the group that would come to be called Union Democrats—in outrage. Douglas, in failing health, became one such Union Democrat.

The events in Charleston Harbor delivered Lincoln from the uncertain start of his presidency. "All the troubles and anxieties of his life had not equalled those which intervened between his Inauguration and the fall of Sumter," Orville Browning remembered Lincoln telling him. On April 15 he called out seventy-five thousand state militiamen—he was dependent on the states to provide him with men—and summoned Congress into emergency session. Two days later Virginia seceded. On behalf of the Confederacy, Virginia militiamen occupied the Harpers Ferry arsenal, close to Washington.

On April 19 Lincoln issued a blockade proclamation, declaring that he would seize not only vessels carrying a Confederate flag, but all those bringing goods into Southern ports. Even though the U.S. Navy consisted of only forty-two ships, the beginnings of Gideon Welles's blockade system were put in place. But with the army, Lincoln ran up against the problem that, like much of the Federal bureaucracy, it had been Southern dominated. Robert E. Lee of the Second Cavalry was approached by the Blair family, by General Scott, and indirectly by Lincoln himself, but then defected to the South anyway. Mary Todd Lincoln's own brother-in-law, an experienced officer named Benjamin Helm, married to Mary's half-sister, Emilie, also went to the South. Col. John Magruder of the artillery assured Lincoln in a visit to the White House on April 18 that he remained loyal, yet three days later he left for service with the Confederacy. It was to be expected—in much of the South, loyalty to the state superseded loyalty to the Union.

While Willie and Tad tore around the White House, and Mary began talking to its Southern-leaning Scots head gardener, John Watt, about the garden and the deplorable state of the decor, Lincoln waited for troops to arrive to protect the wide-open capital. John Nicolay, Lincoln's secretary, focusing his telescope from the White House on buildings in Alexandria, just across the Potomac, a virtual suburb, saw the flag of the Confederacy flying there. When the first regiment to come to the president's aid, the Sixth Massachusetts, detrained in Baltimore, they were attacked by a secessionist mob, and some of the bluecoats were killed by rioters. A Baltimore delegation to the White House asked that troops not be routed through their city, but Lincoln declared, "If I grant you this concession, you will be back here tomorrow, demanding that none shall be marched around it." Nonetheless he did begin to think of alternative routes. After all, pro-Southern Maryland militiamen had torn up large sections of the line outside Baltimore. The capital was sandwiched between a state that had seceded, Virginia, and another, Maryland, that might secede at any time.

The government began handing out large sums of money to enable private contractors to ship troops and acquire armaments for the capital, but by late April, Lincoln, addressing the Sixth Massachusetts at the White House, said, "*You* are the only northern realities." The next day the Seventh New York arrived, and from then on so many other state regiments that it became impossible to move on the White House lawn for military bands. The former law clerk in Lincoln's office, Elmer Ellsworth, to whom Lincoln had been very close, turned up at the White House with his own squad of Zouaves—that is, men dressed in the manner of French infantry in Algeria. Ellsworth's tasseled red cap, red shirt, bloomery trousers, sword, Bowie knife, and revolver were all great hits with Willie and Tad. The sudden appearance of this boy from Springfield, ready to defend the capital, was wonderful for the Lincoln family's morale. Clowning with musket drill in the East Room, he accidentally broke a windowpane, to the amusement of Lincoln's secretaries and sons.

People still muttered about Lincoln's policy of drift, but no one could deny the hours he put in, walking from the family's quarters in the West Wing, through a melee of visitors in the central hall, and into his office on the eastern side of the house. Nicolay had organized matters so that his own office, a writing room, a reception room, and the vestibule were all wrapped protectively around Lincoln's office and the cabinet room. John Hay complained that he and Nicolay and others tried to "erect barriers to defend him against constant interruption, but the president himself was always the first to break them down."

In the South at that time, for the sake of morale and recruiting, Jefferson Davis was visiting all the states of the Confederacy in turn. Lincoln could never find the time away from his desk, or if he was not at his desk, from the telegraph office of the War Department just across the White House lawn. People were astonished, nonetheless, by the ease of access the president offered. He even held levees to which members of the public could come and express their concerns. Lincoln called these receptions his "public opinion baths." But it was not entirely a matter of acquainting himself with public opinion. Office seekers still besieged him. The best positions, as regards patronage, were associated with the directorships of the four thousand U.S. customs houses. The position of collector of the Port of New York, for example, carried a salary of six thousand dollars and the capacity to earn another twenty-five thousand dollars a year in commissions or even in graft. Those who had delivered even the smallest parcel of votes to Abraham Lincoln now looked for their reward on this earth. He told one friend that he thought sometimes the only way he could escape applicants for appointments would be to take a rope and hang himself from one of the trees on the South Lawn. Or else, he added to one of his secretaries, he could move his office to a smallpox hospital.

That spring Lincoln generated great Democratic hostility in the North by suspending habeas corpus and restricting freedom of the press, contrary to his most profoundly held principles. Washington itself harbored a considerable number of spies and many Southern sympathizers. Lincoln wished to make it possible for the army to arrest saboteurs, such as those who burned down the bridge over the Susquehanna, and hold them under military jurisdiction. But more dangerous than the burned-out bridge and wrecked rails, which made the movement of Federal troops impossible, was the fact that the Maryland legislature had met in special session at Annapolis to consider secession. Gen. Benjamin Butler of Massachusetts put Annapolis under martial law, and the Maryland legislature, seeing that secession would mean immediate battle in the streets of their cities, particularly in Baltimore, voted against joining the Confederacy. Lincoln emphasized to Gov. Thomas Hicks of Maryland and to the mayor of Baltimore that he would not countenance their failure to give Federal troops safe passage through Baltimore.

Missouri had also been saved by the quick action of Unionists, including that of the short-lived but heroic Gen. Nathaniel Lyon, who refused to surrender the Federal arsenal in St. Louis.

As for Kentucky, a crucial border state, if it "made no demonstration of force against the United States," he promised, "he would not molest her." He emphasized that he had no designs on the slaves of the border states—indeed he had no constitutional power over them, nor did he have a mandate from the people. If Kentucky went, he knew, the Confederacy would abut right against the southern border of Illinois, and Cairo, the strategic point where the Mississippi joined the Ohio, would probably fall to it. Lincoln is reported as saying that he would like to have God on his side, but he must have Kentucky. Eventually Kentucky declared its neutrality, and Lincoln respected that neutrality publicly, even while turning a blind eye to the fact that Union officers went to that state to raise loyal militias. In September, Confederate forces attacked Kentucky from the direction of Tennessee and occupied the Cumberland Gap. The state ended its neutrality and immediately called for forty thousand volunteers for the Union army.

Suddenly and with a shock, Lincoln lost young Elmer

Ellsworth. Now a colonel, Elmer had led a regiment across the Potomac to Alexandria to occupy that town, and had been hauling down a Confederate flag from the top of Marshal's Tavern when the proprietor shot him dead. "[H]is power to command men was surpassingly great," a grieving Lincoln wrote to Ellsworth's parents. Mary and Lincoln went down to the Washington Navy Yard to visit his body, and somebody gave Mary the blood-splattered Confederate flag for which he had given his life. In the meantime, as Union troops occupied forts around Washington and prepared not only to defend the capital but to make forays into the Virginia hinterland, Stephen A. Douglas took to a sickbed in Chicago and died, forty-seven years old. He had nobly guaranteed a certain Northern Democratic support for Lincoln and the Union. But now that he was gone, would that phalanx of support remain?

Lincoln's bewilderment had arisen and still arose from the fact that there were no precedents for the situation in which he and his cabinet found themselves. The bureaucracies were too small, and the War Department could not accommodate or keep records of all the regiments arriving that spring and early summer in Washington. But their ambitious and earnest commanders would come to see Lincoln, who would have to tell Cameron to give them and their men official status. Many people pestered him for commands as well, including his old dueling opponent, the Irishman General Shields.

Though he said frequently that this was a war to save the Union, not free the slaves, he backed General Butler, stationed at Fort Monroe on the Virginia coast, when he refused to return fugitive slaves to Virginian property owners. The Fugitive Slave Law did not apply to those who were in rebellion against the

United States, said Lincoln. This was emancipation by administrative decision, and word of it penetrated deep into the Confederacy, outraging white Southerners and encouraging young slaves to approach the Union lines.

Before it had been fully safe to do so, and even before Ellsworth's death, Mary began visiting New York to buy new fabrics and items of decor for the run-down White House. Alexander Stewart, New York's greatest merchant, had given a dinner party in her honor, and Mary ordered two thousand dollars' worth of rugs and curtains from him in a single day. She would make eleven such buying trips during her tenure at the White House, and to help moderate her spending, a young man named William S. Wood, appointed acting commissioner of public buildings, was ordered to accompany her. (By June 1861, on top of his other causes of grief, Lincoln received an anonymous letter about Mary's relationship with Wood, implying that it was adulterous. Ever jealous of Lincoln, Mary was capable of—at least—a marked flirtatiousness herself.)

Mary was not the only one, however, who found the White House in deplorable condition. One secretary thought it looked like "an old and unsuccessful hotel." Another wrote, "The East Room has a faded, untidy look, despite its frescoing and its glittering chandeliers. Its paint and furniture need renewing; but so does everything else in the house, within and without." The State Dining Room could not serve more than ten with matched china, and if Lincoln had better things to think of, Mary did not.

After complaining about Lincoln's policy vacuum, Seward forged his own hard-line foreign policy with Britain, threatening Her Majesty's Government with war if it continued to receive Confederate commissioners. To help temper Seward's occasional exuberance, Lincoln involved the handsome and fashionable Sen. Charles Sumner of Massachusetts as his foreign policy adviser. Sumner, a check-trousered dandy but serious-minded, was an expert on British politics, and thus provided a balance for Seward's tendency to bait Westminster. Lincoln became a close friend of both Sumner and Seward. The relationship with thin, beak-nosed Secretary of State Seward, who had so dearly wanted the Republican nomination yet who seemed to have accepted his defeat with grace, was helped by the fact that Seward lived on the corner of Lafayette Square, in the house nearest the west gate of the President's House. Seward and Lincoln would go for walks together, share stories, laugh effusively. They were comrades not only in the preservation of the Union but in that Seward also had a difficult, depressive wife he could not quite figure out.

As for the structured parts of the day, after hours of attending to correspondence, at ten o'clock each morning Lincoln had the doors of his reception room thrown open and met contractors, generals making a case for their militia brigades to be inducted and recognized by the War Department, mothers who told him that their sons were underage or ill and should be let go from the military, officers' wives flirting with him to enhance their husbands' chances. Though he was a faithful husband, he was susceptible to flirtatious and good-looking women, and Mary sensed and resented it. Noon on Tuesdays and Thursdays had always been the official cabinet-meeting hour, but Lincoln was not a regular convener of his cabinet. He not infrequently called in the appropriate cabinet member when a policy issue came up for decision.

He had a fascination with weaponry, and took John Hay to watch the test firings of the massive Dahlgren gun in the Potomac. He would test new breech-loading rifles at a range maintained for him in the Treasury Park beyond the South Lawn of the White House.

At four o'clock each afternoon he would generally go for a carriage ride, often with Mary, unless she was away or ill, in which case he would take Seward or some other old Whig. He would sometimes go to the forts around Washington, or over into northern Virginia, and talk with the men of the army as they prepared their evening meals. If not out in the evenings, or having to host a state dinner, he would work, as the smell of Washington's new sanitary arrangements came up from the swampy canal and the Potomac flats. John Hay said this dangerous stench was worse than that of "twenty thousand drowned cats."

The Lincolns liked to spend their summers at the Returned Soldiers' Home, to the northwest of Washington. Here they were above the pocket of heat that settled in the city, and away from the pestilences of the river and the Washington Canal, and Lincoln commuted to the city by carriage.

11

PRESSURE WAS MOUNTING now for the Union army to go forward and come to grips with Gen. Pierre G. Beauregard's Confederates. Horace Greeley's *New-York Tribune* ran the headline FORWARD TO RICHMOND! seven days in a row, as if to get things started. There had been a strong supposition, even on the part of Washington people, that the war would be over in ninety days—the length of enlistment of the Union volunteers—and expiring enlistments were a further factor in the cry for the battle to be fought.

July 1861 would be Lincoln's first experience of the dilatoriness of generals, in this case, of Gen. Irvin McDowell. McDowell pleaded the inexperience of his troops. "You are green, it is true," said Lincoln, "but they are green also; you are all green alike." Union generals would need to get used to such urgings from the president.

Thanks to Washington spies, including particularly helpful intelligence provided by a Southern sympathizer, the Washington hostess Mrs. Rose Greenhow, Beauregard knew about McDowell's movements and intentions. The two armies faced each other along the banks of a stream called Bull Run near the rail depot of Manassas Junction, Virginia, where new brigades of Confederates from the valley had recently detrained to build up the Rebel army. The coming battle of green troops against green troops would really be a battle for control not only of terrain but of a railhead—the very medium of transportation in which the president himself had developed such expertise as a lawyer. On July 21 citizens who had come out in carriages to observe the battle saw the Union troops go forward over Bull Run with considerable dash. It proved to be a chaotic encounter, however. The Union regiments' experience of Confederate artillery, sited in the fields around the Henry House, ended any illusion people had that this would be a short and near-bloodless affair. Unit cohesion had been poor in the early assaults and broke up almost totally in retreat and flight toward Centreville and Washington. Lincoln's appalled, obstreperous, and morally whipped army was by morning milling and lolling in the streets of the capital, utterly directionless.

Edwin M. Stanton, the lawyer with whom Lincoln had worked on an agricultural machinery patent case, and who would be secretary of war before the year was out, wrote, "The capture of Washington now seems to be inevitable—during the whole of Monday and Tuesday it might have been taken without any resistance. The rout, overthrow, and utter demoralization of the whole army is complete."

Lincoln had been up till after midnight on the evening of the battle, in the War Department across the green from the President's Park, receiving catastrophic telegrams. As he went home to the White House, Sens. Zachariah Chandler and Benjamin Wade, who had been spectators and had drawn their own revolvers to try to prevent soldiers from fleeing, arrived at Lincoln's door with outraged tales of the cowardice of his soldiers. Then General Scott himself came to the White House at two o'clock to insist that Mary Lincoln and her sons leave the city immediately for their own safety. To her credit, Mary refused. Lincoln declared a national fast day, "a day of humiliation, prayer and fasting for all the people of the nation," to attract a larger measure of divine beneficence toward the Union forces than had hitherto been noticeable.

In the aftermath the press called for the appointment of a young, brilliant West Pointer and railroad executive, George B. McClellan, seventeen years younger than Lincoln, who had devised a plan for the securing of the Ohio River line in the middle, an advance through Virginia on Richmond on the right, and the capture of Nashville on the left. For this plan, designed in conjunction with the navy to crush the South economically, he was raised to the rank of major general and made commander of the Department of the Ohio. However, in this position, McClellan, a devout Democrat, went further than Lincoln would have liked in pledging to return the slaves even of secessionists, and using the army to do it. But the success of McClellan's troops in driving small Confederate forces out of western Virginia helped lay the basis for the badly needed, breakaway Unionist state of West Virginia. Desperate for a leader after the whipping at Bull Run, the president and the War Department summoned him to Washington to take over the Department of the Potomac.

McClellan had a robust ego, which saw a due deference to his own great talents in the president's tentative manner. His attitude toward Lincoln would, from a week after Bull Run, be marked by a contempt McClellan would progressively take fewer and fewer pains to hide. "Isn't he a rare bird?" he would soon ask a fellow Union general as the president left a meeting.

McClellan was organizationally brilliant and ambitious. The

day after the battle Lincoln had signed a bill authorizing the enlistment of five hundred thousand three-year volunteers. McClellan was the brain who would organize, supply, and enthuse them. He built up a set of powerful fortifications around the capital, formed the patriotic volunteer regiments into a new, well-drilled system of brigades and divisions, and endeared himself to the soldiery by giving them confidence. He wanted no interference from the aged General Scott, and would ultimately maneuver him into resigning, clearing the way for his own almost immediate appointment as general in chief. His competence was so great that the whole Union seemed dependent on him, and this—as at least one historian says—gave him a Messiah complex.

He was politically soft on slavery. He also believed with the president that this was a war against the slave-owning class, not against ordinary Southerners, and he shared with Lincoln as well the delusion that there was in fact a Unionist majority among the people of the South whom the Southern aristocracy had tricked into secession. Once Union arms began to prevail, this Unionist mass would rise against the slave owners. McClellan was delighted to know that Lincoln, also, did not see himself as fighting an abolition war but a war to save the Union.

Having built an army in short order, McClellan dallied in moving it against the Confederates in northern Virginia. He feared that General Beauregard had prodigious numbers, 450,000 men, waiting to spring on him should he cross the Potomac. At the end of September, however, when McClellan did send units across, they found Quaker guns, "wooden models." Embarrassed, the Young Napoleon risked committing a small Union force over the river north of Washington.

On the eve of this endeavor, Mary and Abraham Lincoln entertained on the lawn of the White House one of Lincoln's old Illinois friends and rivals, after whom he and Mary had named their lost son, Eddie. Edward Baker, now a colonel commanding a raw brigade, was exhilarated at the prospect of the coming action. The next day, upriver near Leesburg, Baker's brigade came against a Confederate force posted atop a wooded ridge named Ball's Bluff, and, among seventeen hundred casualties, Baker was killed. Thus, two of Lincoln's favorite friends had died in Union gestures beyond the Potomac. Ball's Bluff certainly cured McClellan of trying any further projects that fall.

His elevation to general in chief on November 5 increased his streak of hubris. "I can do it all," he famously wrote. If anything, McClellan became even more scornful of Lincoln, whom he called "the giraffe." "He was not a man of very strong character," McClellan wrote of Lincoln, "and he was destitute of refinement—certainly in no sense a gentleman—he was easily wrought upon by the coarse associates whose style of conversation agreed so well with his own." McClellan hated the president's parables.

One night, Lincoln, his friend Secretary of State Seward, and his secretary John Hay waited at General McClellan's rented house for him to come in. The general returned from a wedding and, entering his home by a side entrance, was told about the distinguished guests waiting for him. McClellan went to bed, leaving them sitting in his parlor. On the way home Hay told the president this was "unparalleled impudence," but Lincoln advised him that it was best at a time like this not to worry about etiquette or personal dignity. Nonetheless he stopped attending on McClellan and from then on, unless visiting him in the field, would summon his general to the White House.

McClellan was predictably outraged when the president and other members of the cabinet began to suspect his tales of being continually outnumbered. Having read sundry works on strategy, the president presented his own plan, named the Occoquan Plan after the strategic little town in northern Virginia, and involving two columns attacking the Confederate heartland. As he argued it, "Both points will probably not be successfully resisted at the same time." McClellan, however, said his own new plan was nearly ready. As McClellan delayed in the East, out in the West another general, Don Carlos Buell, told the War Department that he could not invade eastern Tennessee, where it was believed the pro-Union piedmont and mountain people would rise in large numbers against the Confederacy. The railways were inadequate for the task of transporting his men, said Buell. And so the year drew to its close.

But not without its having been a very difficult December. Mary had gathered around herself a salon of fashionable and racy men with whom she met in the Blue Room, one of the three parlors of the White House—"My beau monde friends of the Blue Room," she called this group. It consisted of Governor Newell of New Jersey, Assistant Secretary of the Navy Fox, and a remarkable fellow called the Chevalier Wikoff. Henry Wikoff was not only a former British agent but a friend of every notable European political figure, from Austria's Klemens von Metternich to Great Britain's prime minister, Lord Palmerston, to Camillo di Cavour, one of the leaders of the movement for Italian unification. He had also spent time in an Italian prison for abducting an heiress, an experience he had turned into a best-selling book. He carried with him the glamour of places more remarkable and elegant than either Springfield, Illinois, or Washington, D.C. He was also able to persuade the press, notably the *New York Herald,* the best-selling newspaper of its day, to praise Mrs. Lincoln's social skills, presence, and charm.

In December the text of an as-yet-embargoed presidential address to Congress appeared in the *New York Herald.* Congress suspected, as Abraham must have, that Wikoff had somehow gotten it from Mary Lincoln. This offered a great chance for vengeance to all those who disliked Mary for her extravagant refurbishing of the White House, her taste for Empress Eugénie–style dresses, and her supposed influence over Lincoln. The House Judiciary Committee summoned Wikoff, in the hope he would confirm that Mary Todd Lincoln had leaked the speech.

Mary was vulnerable to a degree that could have created a disabling national scandal. She had, for example, entered into an arrangement with Watt, the head gardener of the White House, to pad the books on wages and nursery expenses, creating on one occasion a largely fictional purchase of one thousand dollars' worth of seeds and splitting the sum with him. She still suffered, as one of Lincoln's secretaries noticed, from an astonishing polarity of impulses. Her extravagance on furnishings and dresses would be succeeded by sudden panic attacks of frugality, when she tried to sell the manure from the White House stables as a buffer against coming postpresidential poverty. All this might now be revealed by the Judiciary Committee, if Wikoff would identify his source for the speech he had sent to the *Herald.*

Another member of the Blue Room salon, Gen. Dan Sickles, a gifted New York Democratic operator who had, the year before Lincoln's election, shot his wife's lover dead outside the White House and been acquitted, left his brigade on the Potomac and came to town to defend Wikoff. Sickles skillfully shifted the blame for the leaked document to the head gardener, threatening him with prosecution for his embezzlement if he did not accept responsibility for the purloined speech. Watt did so, and Lincoln and Mary were saved acute embarrassment. Mary was able to go on to redecorate the White House by means both earnest and crafty. And her seamstress, Lizzie Keckley, a liberated slave, supplied her with dresses made of the finest fabrics for the winter season.

On the international level, December 1861 was also fraught. An overzealous commander in the U.S. Navy intercepted the British vessel *Trent* on the open sea and took off it two Confederate commissioners who were on their way to London. The British were outraged by this high-handed act and dispatched redcoats by the thousands to Canada, in case it became necessary to declare war on the United States. For a time it looked as though the Union would be fighting on two fronts—against the Confederacy and the British—and as much as that delighted certain enemies of Britain, such as Navy Secretary Welles and Secretary of State Seward, and as much as the Irish in the Union army were excited by the prospect, Lincoln was desperate to get the incident behind him. His constituents, however, would not forgive him if he simply backed down before Lord Palmerston. Lincoln gathered his cabinet in a special meeting at the White House on Christmas Day at which, on the basis of McClellan's advice that the Union could not win against both the Rebels and the British, the administration reluctantly agreed to release the Rebel commissioners, James Mason and John Slidell, to continue their journey.

One benefit of the new year would be that Simon Cameron, under a shadow for the way he awarded military contracts, was persuaded to become minister to St. Petersburg. Lincoln could finally replace him with Edwin Stanton, the famed attorney and former Buchanan cabinet member who had once treated Abraham with some dismissiveness in a patent case in Cincinnati over reapers. Lincoln's gift for letting go of grudges would be rewarded, for Stanton became a loyal and gifted secretary of war.

Over Christmas and New Year's, Lincoln pressed his own strategic plan for the prosecution of the great conclusive campaign against the Rebels. Stung, McClellan at last produced a revised plan of his own—a movement toward New Orleans, an attack on Georgia, and, for the Army of the Potomac, a shift south, down the Chesapeake Bay to Urbanna on the Rappahannock. This would outflank the Confederates at Manassas and enable Richmond to be captured.

There were generals in the West doing positive things. A fellow Illinois man, former West Pointer, store manager, and problem drinker, Ulysses Simpson Grant, took his men along the Tennessee River, backed by a flotilla of gunboats, and captured Fort Henry. Ten days later his force seized Fort Donaldson on the Cumberland River. This put the Confederacy in retreat, out of western Kentucky and western Tennessee. Gen. Don Carlos Buell captured Nashville on February 28, Gen. Samuel R. Curtis defeated the Rebels in Arkansas, and Gen. John Pope—one of the officers who had escorted Lincoln across the country to his inauguration—captured New Madrid and set siege to Island

Number Ten on the Mississippi. Not long after, on April 6, General Grant was attacked, and with some skill he fought a great and bitter battle at Shiloh on the Tennessee, a two-day affair involving twenty thousand casualties in total, at the close of which the Confederates withdrew. The Rebels' resistance had been so horrifying that it convinced Grant that there would be no easy settlement to the conflict, and that the only viable basis for a peace would be the unconditional surrender of the secessionist states.

In early February 1862 Mary Lincoln enjoyed a grand moment as a hostess, having organized a magnificent party in the White House. The *Washington Star* said it was "the most superb affair of its kind ever seen." But the Lincolns' son Willie was upstairs with a terrible fever. Two weeks after this night of nights, Willie died—possibly of typhoid fever from the foul waters into which the district's burst sewage mains had flowed. He had been Mary's favorite, as little Tad, with his speech defect and hyperactivity, was Lincoln's. Not that Lincoln himself had anything other than an intense love for the precocious Willie, who could call out train timetables and name connecting railroads all the way from Chicago to Boston.

Mary found it almost impossible to absorb Willie's death. Lincoln would come to worry about her sanity, and for its sake, he allowed her to take part in séances in the hope that she might communicate with Willie again. Mediums, such as a charlatan named Lord Colchester, were admitted to the Red Room of the White House, where they would go into trances in which dead Union generals supposedly returned to give the president advice. Lincoln bore their advice and flimflam bravely, tolerating the presence of the mediums for Mary's sake. It was of course an era when spiritism, "spirit-rapping," was a widespread enthusiasm even among members of the cabinet. Mary's seamstress, Lizzie Keckley, believed readily that the dead could return with messages, and did little to dissuade Mary. And Lincoln himself was grateful for the help of Gen. Dan Sickles, who sometimes accompanied Mary to séances and kept an eye on her. Again, the preposterous behavior of the grief-afflicted Mary attracted comment.

The successes in the West made Lincoln and others believe that one masterstroke in Virginia would win Richmond and bring the rebellion to a close. But even Lincoln began to believe, as McClellan delayed, that some Democratic generals didn't really want anything drastic to happen to the Confederacy, fearing that a great victory would encourage the administration to emancipate slaves. When McClellan did probe across the river on March 9, again finding Quaker guns in considerable number, the congressional Joint Committee for the Conduct of the War demanded the man's dismissal. Lincoln was not ready to do so, since a definite plan of attack was about to be implemented.

But the grounds for McClellan's trying to outflank the Confederates by going to Urbanna no longer existed—the Confederates had abandoned Manassas Junction. So the Young Napoleon decided to move his army even farther down the coast, to Fort Monroe. It was a good plan, for Fort Monroe was southeast of Richmond, and at the tip of the peninsula up which McClellan intended to move rapidly on the Confederate capital. But instead of doing that, he frittered his men away in a siege of Yorktown. Lincoln and Salmon P. Chase had come down to Fort

Monroe early in the campaign, late April to early May, to see what was holding McClellan up. "I think it is the precise time for you to strike a blow," Lincoln advised him:

> By delay the enemy will relatively gain upon you. . . . You will do me the justice to remember I always insisted, that going down the Bay in search of a field, instead of fighting at or near Manassas, was only shifting, and not surmounting, a difficulty—that you would find the same enemy, and the same or equal intrenchments, at either place. . . . I beg to assure you that I've never written you, or spoken to you, in greater kindness of feeling than now, nor with a fuller purpose to sustain you, so far as is in my most anxious judgment. I consistently can. *But you must act.*

McClellan sulked about this urging, and told his wife, "I was much tempted to reply that he had better come and do it himself."

Though by the end of May, on the edge of the swamps of the Chickahominy River, McClellan won a great battle at Fair Oaks, a position from which his scouts, climbing trees, could see the domes and steeples of Richmond, he then let his men stand still a month in their encampments in the turpentine forests, ensuring that many of them would succumb to malaria, typhus, and dysentery.

As McClellan tarried, a former Union colonel, now a Confederate general, by the name of Robert E. Lee took over command of the Rebel troops on the peninsula. McClellan persuaded himself that he was so outnumbered by Lee that his best option now was to save his army. Thus he ordered a retreat away from

Richmond down to Harrison's Landing on the James River, from which Union shipping could protect and resupply his men.

The astonishing impertinence of an accusatory letter McClellan wrote the president, late at night on the retreat to Harrison's Landing, appalled even Lincoln. "I know that a few thousand men more would have changed this battle from a defeat to a victory—as it is the Govt. must not and cannot hold me responsible for the result. . . . If I save this army now I tell you plainly that I owe no thanks to you or any other persons in Washington—you have done your best to sacrifice this Army." McClellan's excuse for adopting this tone was based in part on a telegram Lincoln sent on July 1, telling him that he could not be reinforced "for your present emergency. . . . If you are not strong enough to face the enemy you must find a place of security, and wait, rest, and repair."

McClellan's accusation was that Lincoln had deliberately kept back reserves around Washington, whereas the truth was that the president had done his best to strip the Washington defenses down to twenty-six thousand men. In the face of these accusations, Lincoln again showed enormous forbearance, some of which may have been caused by the fact that the army loved McClellan and might help him in a march on Washington and the declaration of a benign dictatorship. Lincoln was convinced, though, that

if by magic he could reinforce McClellan with 100,000 men today, he [McClellan] would be in ecstasy over it, thank him for it, and tell him that he would go to Richmond tomorrow; but that when tomorrow came he would telegraph that he had information that the enemy had 400,000 men and that he could not advance without reinforcements.

Lincoln came down by steamer again to visit McClellan, this time at Harrison's Landing. But by now the only option, particularly given McClellan's frame of mind, was to withdraw. For, having saved their capital, Lee and Stonewall Jackson intended to go rampaging northward toward Manassas again. Though many wanted McClellan sacked, Lincoln still wondered about the potential effect on the army. He made a concession to his cabinet by taking overall command away from McClellan and making the dour Henry Halleck, "Old Brains" to the troops, general in chief.

12

BY MEANS OF forced marches, Lee was back in northern Virginia again. Only the earliest returning fragments of the Army of the Potomac were made grudgingly available by McClellan for General Pope's Army of Virginia, which was charged with stopping the fast-moving Rebels. Pope was despised by the Young Napoleon. He was a Republican, and had been one of the president's bodyguards from Springfield to Washington.

The Rebels attacked him at Manassas, and Pope failed to perform well, losing sixteen thousand casualties and leaving Lee and Jackson free to threaten Washington. In September 1862, following Pope's defeat, Attorney General Bates described Lincoln as being "in deep distress . . . wrung by the bitterest anguish." The cabinet was united yet again in wanting McClellan dismissed for his unhelpfulness and his willingness to let Pope "get out of his trouble alone." But still Lincoln would not accede. He believed there were serious doubts that the army would fight for anyone other than McClellan. Lincoln was in a sense the general's prisoner. Soon the Young Napoleon was reluctantly returned to full command of both the Army of the Potomac and the Army of Virginia.

The victory of Lee's Confederates at Second Manassas left the way open to the first Rebel advance into the North. Lincoln was delighted to hear that Lee and Jackson's forces had crossed the Potomac and were somewhere in western Maryland, on the flank of the capital. He saw it as a great chance for McClellan to get between them and their bases, cut them off, and fight them on ground of the Union's choosing. McClellan was not seized by any such excitement and, moving edgily west to cut off the Rebels, got an extraordinary advantage when two of his soldiers found a copy of Lee's orders wrapped around two cigars under a tree near Frederick, Maryland. Typically, however, he did not quite believe his luck, and still marched slowly. In dispatches he estimated that Lee's army consisted of one hundred twenty thousand men, which proved to be nearly three times its actual size.

As Abraham haunted the telegraph office at Stanton's War Department, the two armies encountered each other along a creek called Antietam and in front of the little town of Sharpsburg, forty miles northwest of Washington. McClellan authorized his first attack in the early predawn of September 17. It was all unutterably savage, a battle fought in intimate, cramped venues—in the thickets of the East and West Woods, in the Cornfield, around the plain chapel and in the fields of a German Pacifist sect named the Dunkers, along Bloody Lane, and across two little bridges which spanned the creek and led into Sharpsburg. Masses of men engaged each other at close range. The opposing artillery corps blew clumps of men out of the lines. By nine-thirty in the morning, twelve thousand men had been killed and wounded, and by late afternoon that figure mounted to some twenty-three thousand.

By twilight, although it could be said that both sides had fought to a standstill, the Union had Lee's men caught in a pocket around Sharpsburg, with the Potomac at their back. Lincoln knew that the enemy could have been obliterated the next day, but McClellan made his troops sit where they were, and on the night of September 18, the Confederates crossed the Potomac and returned south with only the lightest interference. Lincoln urged McClellan to cross the Potomac and get between Lee and the Rebel capital:

> If we cannot beat him when he bears the wastage of coming to us, we never can when we bear the wastage of going to him. . . . As we must beat him somewhere, or fail finally, we can do it, if at all, easier near to us than far away. . . . It is all easy if our troops march as well as the enemy; and it is unmanly to say they cannot do it.

Visiting McClellan and walking around the immense Federal camp with his old friend from Illinois, Orville Browning, Abraham pointed to the vast array of tents and bivouacs and said, in a tone of patient but melancholy sarcasm, "That is General McClellan's bodyguard." McClellan claimed that he could not pursue Lee because his cavalry horses were "broken down from fatigue." Lincoln wired back, "Will you pardon me for asking what the horses of your army have done since the battle of Antietam that fatigue anything?"

But, ever cooperative, by October 27 Lincoln recorded that he had sent nearly eight thousand new cavalry horses and remarked with his usual incisiveness in a memorandum to McClellan that if they were not rested now, when would they ever be?

Despite the fact that McClellan would not pursue and destroy Lee, Lincoln still had the rare Union victory of Antietam, which would serve as the basis for his first Emancipation Proclamation. He called a cabinet meeting for September 21 to discuss and find new means to alleviate anguish in the homes of the North, and to raise the often-canvassed matter of emancipation.

When, in July 1862, Secretary of War Stanton and his young wife lost an infant child, James, Lincoln attended the funeral, and on the way back to the White House in a carriage with Seward and Welles, told them that he had "come to the conclusion that we must free the slaves or be ourselves subdued." The war had taken away the constitutional restrictions regarding freeing the slaves in Rebel communities. They could be freed as a matter of military necessity under the president's war powers.

Soon after that discussion Montgomery Blair had warned Lincoln that the troops would resent any move to turn the war to save the Union into a war to free slaves, while Salmon Chase thought the proclamation Lincoln had in mind was far too soft. Lincoln had to reconcile and temper these opinions into cabinet approval of a final document. The September 21 cabinet meeting began interestingly and with a typical Lincoln flourish, part cunning, part naïveté. The president started off by reading the perplexed cabinet a chapter out of *A High Handed Outrage in Utica* by his favorite comic writer and performer, Artemus Ward. Many in the cabinet were more bemused than amused, and in that atmosphere, Lincoln presented his draft Emancipation Proclamation for comment.

The document offered the border states a scheme of compensated emancipation, followed by an "effort to colonize persons of African descent, with their consent, upon this continent or elsewhere." Apart from that it declared that if the Rebels did not return to the Union by January 1, 1863, Lincoln would free "thenceforward and forever" all slaves in the Rebel states. The army and navy would recognize the freedom of slaves in the South. Most of the cabinet supported Lincoln, even though some of them thought the proclamation might have a dangerous impact on groups of people in the North, in the army, and in the border states. It was published the following day.

While some abolitionists applauded the proclamation as an opening gambit, and Ralph Waldo Emerson called it "an event worth the dreadful war," others mocked it, for all that Lincoln had done was to liberate the slaves his armies had not so far encountered. He realized that this could leave the proclamation open to mockery, and some abolitionists at one end of the scale, and many Democratic newspapers and orators at the other, obliged him. He was accused too of inciting slave uprisings in the South.

One of the effects of the proclamation, however, was to put paid to any plan the British Cabinet had of recognizing the South. Lincoln had given the war a moral dimension the British could not gainsay. Thus Antietam had had its double impact— a military and a moral victory. This did not stop McClellan from reminding his soldiers in a grudging order to his army that any mistakes by the executive (he meant the proclamation) could be corrected at the polls in the coming midterm elections. McClellan felt outraged at being the unwitting catalyst of the proclamation.

Harrowed and hollowed out by the weight of decision and blood, Lincoln had, in the two years since Brady had taken his photograph in New York, aged ten. A number of witnesses mention how stooped he was. The grief in his eyes had taken on an irremediable depth. He was "hypo" ravaged. And yet, despite his agnosticism, he had come to believe in God as a historic force. "In great contests each party claims to act in accordance with the will of God. Both may be, but one must be wrong. God cannot be for and against the same thing at the same time. In the present civil war it is quite possible that God's purpose is something different from the purpose of either party; and yet the human instrumentalities, working just as they do, are the best adaptation to effect his purpose."

On November 7 Lincoln at last relieved McClellan of command. Though, as the president had feared, a number of officers told him to march on Washington and make himself dictator, McClellan did not do so. He believed that he would become the Democratic presidential candidate in 1864, by which time he expected the Republicans to be in such bad odor that he could be elected as a national savior. In fact he went so far as to urge his men to give his successor the same loyalty they had given him. That successor was Gen. Ambrose Burnside, a robust six-footer with ferocious "sideburns," as people had begun to call those flourishes of facial hair in whimsical regard for the general. He had been approached earlier to replace McClellan, and had pleaded not to be given the job. Underneath his West Point braggadocio, he possessed an edgy, haunted soul.

The North punished the administration for emancipation, and for the terrible casualties of the war, in the elections of 1862. The North's five big states—New York, Pennsylvania, Ohio, Illinois, and Indiana—went to the Democrats, as did New Jersey. The Republicans were forced into coalition with border

Unionists and so retained control of Congress by a slim edge. The political tide was bitterly set against Lincoln, and he looked set for defeat in 1864, even if he managed to get the Republican nomination, which seemed unlikely. Despite his gesture of the Emancipation Proclamation, the radical, abolitionist wing of his party disliked his reticence on slavery and his failed pursuit of the war. And in the North now were an army of vocal opponents of the war whom Republicans called Copperheads. They urged immediate peace negotiations, and in the dour winter of 1862–63, when the Union could not find a general to win in Virginia, a negotiated peace seemed an attractive proposition.

In that December's annual message to Congress, Lincoln held out to the battered Union the prospect of a population equal to that of Europe by 1930, in which year he believed, based on projections, the American population could reach 251 million. "And we *will* reach this, too, if we do not ourselves relinquish the chance, by the folly and evils of this Union, and by long and exhausting war springing from the only great element of national discord among us." This coming glory—he saw it unambiguously as such—was a further justification for emancipation. Increasing population would make it easier for the United States to pay compensation for the emancipation of the slaves. He attacked the argument that "free colored persons" would injure and "displace white labor and white laborers." "Is it true, then, that colored persons can displace any more white labor, by being free, than by remaining slaves?" In shortening the war, emancipation would pay for the future colonization of the blacks. The resonating end of that December speech was classic Lincoln oratory. It seems to belong to another age, to the late twentieth, early twenty-first century, say, when speeches have come to be crafted for their one or two memorable, easily quotable sentences. For compared with the oratory of the day, it had qualities of chaste simplicity. "In giving freedom to the *slave* we *assure* freedom to the *free*—honorable alike in what we give, and what we preserve. We shall nobly save, or meanly lose, the last best hope of earth."

December, like the previous December, brought no end to the anguish of Lincoln and the Union. The army had set up its winter quarters on the Rappahannock opposite the town of Fredericksburg, a river port backed by an escarpment. General Burnside permitted the Confederates two or three weeks to dig in on this high ground before he sent the army across to attack Marye's Heights above the town. Division after division was launched piecemeal against the stone walls at the top of the bluff. Men went forward in the certainty of death, some of them—having made arrangements with undertakers in the town for their corpses to be shipped home—with their names pinned to their backs. The Union casualties outnumbered the Confederates by more than three to one. It was a frightful slaughter, and brought grievous news to the hearths of the North just when people thought the year's dangers were over. Burnside broke down weeping at the mayhem he had caused, and Lincoln was again oppressed by the profoundest "hypo."

And besides that, the cabinet was bickering, the florid and rather pietistic Salmon P. Chase encouraged in his own ambitions by the fact that, as one American said, "Nobody believes in him [Lincoln] anymore." As his opening gambit Chase was trying to undermine Seward by having documents and opinions circulated to Republican senators claiming that Seward was not zealous in the prosecution of the war, that he improperly interfered in the business of other cabinet members, and that he did not allow important issues to get a full discussion in cabinet. By depicting Seward in these terms, Chase also cast Lincoln as a man who had no control over Seward. It was a message the Radical Republicans, who believed Lincoln wasn't pursuing the war in the right way, or wasn't sufficiently thoroughgoing about abolition, were willing to accept. Lincoln told his friend Browning, "They wish to get rid of me, and I am half disposed to gratify them." The senators, many of them convinced of Chase's picture of things, were already relaying their complaints to Lincoln.

Lincoln could sometimes look so sheepish and lugubrious that people forgot he was a man of potent political skills. Chase himself had done so. On the evening of December 18, Lincoln invited the Republican senators and the cabinet to his White House office, and put to his entire cabinet, in front of these senatorial witnesses, the questions that had been raised about Seward. Chase was embarrassed when all his fellow cabinet members said they were not aware of Seward's strangling debate or interfering. When asked, Chase himself had to admit that Seward was not the evil genius the senators feared, and of course, as a corollary, affirmed that Lincoln was the leader of his own cabinet. Lincoln typically declared afterward, "If there were any worse Hell than he had been in for two days, he would like to know it." He would frequently make this reference to the sufferings of hell—it was a recurrent image the "hypo" and vicious events forced on him.

Lincoln slept badly on the cold last night of an appalling year. In the morning, since none of the Rebel states had returned to the Union, he would need to issue a confirmatory proclamation, freeing their slaves. There was no victory to reinforce its validity. Out on the Mississippi, U. S. Grant had run into troubles in his plan to take Vicksburg. On all fronts there seemed to be delay and bewilderment. Lincoln knew from early messages received in the War Department telegraph office that a savage battle had just begun at Murfreesboro in Tennessee, at an important crossroads of the Nashville & Chattanooga Railroad.

The president woke early, lit the fire and gaslights in his office, and worked on the final version of the definitive Emancipation Proclamation. There were exemptions to emancipation.

"For the present," parts of Louisiana under Union control; some occupied places in Virginia; areas of West Virginia (in which slave ownership was at a low level in any case); border states such as Maryland, Kentucky, and Missouri, which had remained in the Union; and Tennessee—which was now under Union control and whose people had in large part supported the Union or repented of their secession—were exempt. There the end of slavery would come a little more gradually. As for the rest, all slaves in the Rebel states were now "forever free.... I invoke the considerate judgment of mankind, and the gracious favor of Almighty God." Lincoln urged "the people so declared to be free to abstain from all violence." Former slaves "of suitable condition" would be admitted into the armed service of the United States. The idea of the black Union soldier, frequently promoted by abolitionist Northerners, was now given reality.

Mary liberated herself by giving a White House reception— her first public event since Willie had died. She was in exultant if shaky form. Despite her many Confederate relatives, she was elated at the proclamation, and her favorite son, Robert, had come down from Harvard to be with the family throughout the holidays. Mary survived the reception in a dress of gray silk. She had still not lost her faith in séances and charlatans, some of them genial, some of them vicious. According to Lizzie Keckley, Lincoln had had to point out to Mary the Washington madhouse and warn her gently that if she could not accommodate her grief, that was where she would end. So, even domestically, Lincoln was fighting an uncertain battle.

On the afternoon of New Year's Day, a group of former slaves who had had the proclamation read to them came in joy to the White House lawn, a black preacher related, and called for the president to emerge, so that they could hug him to death. But Lincoln spent considerable time in the telegraph office in the next few days, waiting for news from Murfreesboro, where Gen. William Rosecrans's army, driven north along the banks of Stone's River, yet managed to hold their position and exhaust the enemy's attack. The Rebels withdrew to Chattanooga, and Lincoln, who had been preparing to absorb and explain another Union defeat, was saved that trouble.

Close to home, along the Rappahannock, as Burnside attempted a maneuver against Lee, his wagons bogged axle-deep in mud. It was yet another dispiriting mistake. In the army along the Rappahannock, absenteeism, if not desertion, was now at a prodigious level—even some generals overstayed leave in northern cities. But no one could have shown such certainty and endurance as Lincoln. On January 26 the president invited Joe Hooker, a volatile, boozy, profane West Pointer, whose nickname was Fightin' Joe, to the White House and handed him a letter:

> I have placed you at the head of the Army of the Potomac. . . . I think it best for you to know that there are some things in regard to which, I am not quite satisfied with you. . . . I have heard, in such a way as to believe it, of your recently saying that both the Army and the Government needed a dictator. Of course, it was not *for* this, but in spite of it, that I have given you the command. Only those generals who gain successes, can set up dictators. What I now ask of you is military success, and I will risk the dictatorship.

This tone was characteristic of Lincoln's frankness with generals. He was pleased that Hooker was full of ideas not only about how to defeat Lee but about what he would do once Richmond was captured. But Lincoln would have to wait until the earth dried out in the spring to find out if he had made a good choice.

13

BY THE LATE WINTER of 1863, Lincoln's administration had already transformed the American economy and given it its modern cast. This had been a matter of necessity. At the start of 1862 Lincoln said, "Chase has no money, and he tells me he can raise no more. The bottom is out of the tub." Union defeats in 1861 had caused banks to panic, suspend specie payment, and issue notes of questionable value that left the Treasury short of the means to pay contractors. Lincoln and Chase now initiated measures that, in the old days, with Southern Democrats to deal with, would not have been approved by the House. Indeed, in seceding, the South gave up its domination of policy making. Up to the start of the war, in the seventy-two years of the existence of the United States, a series of Southern slaveholders had occupied the White House for a total of just under fifty years. (After the war it would be a hundred years before a Southerner was elected president.) The South and its upholders also dominated the House and Senate for huge swaths of time, and designed policies to favor the plantation gentry.

Now, free from that dead hand, Lincoln and Chase embarked on a scheme to raise money to fight the war. They authorized the aggressive marketing of government war bonds to ordinary citizens as well as to professional investors. Repaying them, Chase understood, would take more specie than the Treasury possessed, and so, with Lincoln's approval, he introduced into Congress a Legal Tender Act, which permitted the issue of $150 million in paper money. Thus the greenback, that final insult to the old economy under which Lincoln had spent his boyhood, was born, and issued by the Treasury, receivable for all debts public and private. The Jeffersonian idyll, subsistence farmers trading with one another in happy kind, had already been rendered irrelevant by an increasing volume of specie in the country, a few pieces of which, thrown by passengers, had once landed on the boards of Lincoln's cockboat and given him ideas. Now the American Eden was obliterated in a snowstorm of greenbacks. There were many complaints that this phenomenon was contrary to political, moral, and national honor. Greenbacks were condemned as unconstitutional, since the Constitution empowered the Federal government to issue coinage only, but Lincoln demanded the right to issue them under emergency war powers. Some financiers told Lincoln that he had wrecked the country, and that the greenback would cause huge inflation as the war became more expensive. But the war had to be paid for.

Similarly, a flat 3 percent tax on all incomes over eight hundred dollars per year was introduced, and though it produced at first an insubstantial flow of revenue, it marked the beginning of the fiscal world twentieth-century Americans would inherit. A sales tax on a wide range of goods from tobacco to playing cards left people complaining that nothing was left untaxed except the air. Confiscated Southern capital also helped national revenue.

In early 1863 Chase had framed a National Banking Act, for a series of national banks that would handle the issuing of greenbacks. "Finance will rule the country for the next fifty years," declared Lincoln. He was skillful in choosing the right senators to guide the act through the Congress. States' righters feared that the National Bank would centralize the economy and undermine state banks.

Again, without the Southerners in the House to thwart his dream of "internal improvements," Lincoln was able to initiate a transcontinental railroad to the Pacific. After the Pacific Railroad Act was passed, the Central Pacific began laying tracks eastward on January 8, 1863, with the intention of meeting the Union Pacific's line running out of Omaha. Both companies were encouraged by huge land grants.

Southerners had always opposed Homestead Acts for fear they would fill the West with antislavery Northerners. But Lincoln's vision was, plainly stated by himself, "cutting up the wild lands into parcels, so that every poor man may have a home." He didn't account for the reality that speculators would buy out and accumulate land held by struggling freeholders. His Land Grant College Act provided for agricultural colleges—designed to teach the children of farmers "scientific husbandry," how to implement the newest techniques of crop and livestock management, and how to connect the farmer to markets, knowledge that itself was an escape from a merely subsistence life—to be subsidized by the sale of federal lands.

Most of this legislation, passed in 1862 or early 1863, would alter the United States as thoroughly as did Salmon Chase's financial reforms. Other shocks to established norms abounded as well. Throughout the late winter and early spring, black soldiers were recruited by Union officers in the North and in the occupied South. Gen. George H. Thomas formed many black regiments along the Mississippi, thus employing the manpower of escaped slaves and keeping them out of the North. Lincoln wrote to his appointed governor of Tennessee, Andrew Johnson, "The bare sight of 50,000 armed, and drilled black soldiers on the banks of the Mississippi, would end the rebellion at once."

The cabinet was also considering a draft to fill the Union ranks. The use of the draft generated further antiwar rhetoric in the North, and perhaps most acutely in New York City. New York workers of a number of racial backgrounds—especially Irish, German, and Swedish—feared that a flood of liberated slaves would undermine further their already parlous wage conditions. The draft was also condemned as an intrusion by the nation on the desires of the citizen, and as a further violation of Democratic ideology. In fact only fifty thousand men would be drafted, and the wealthy could in any case evade the draft by paying a bounty of three hundred dollars, which was passed on to whoever substituted for them. But the process nevertheless acted as a spur to recruitment and a further sign that the Union intended to finish this war.

Later, in the summer, there would be fierce antidraft riots in New York City; attacks on blacks and even on the downtown black orphanages; assaults on notable Republican households, businesses, and newspapers; and pitched battles between the Union army and working-class people who opposed the draft, a great number of them Irish. Lincoln was appalled to hear of these savage street and tenement confrontations between citizens and the army. But, depressed or not, he was unrelenting. Perhaps the depression and steadfastness were two faces of the one being, and one entailed the other. He had learned from his youth how to endure debilitating self-doubt.

Interestingly, however, there was one young man who for

Mary's sake was exempt both from the draft and from moral pressure to join the crusade. Robert Lincoln remained at Harvard, his mother pleading a slight astigmatism as the reason he could not yet serve. Her husband could see clearly enough that the loss of Robert would send Mary Todd Lincoln over the edge. There was, however, inevitable muttering about the fact that a man so keen to deploy other people's sons was not willing to deploy his own.

In any event, it might have become a moot point, since Fighting Joe Hooker had a wonderful strategic plan to end the war. He would, in the manner of the Confederate Stonewall Jackson, secretly move eighty thousand of his men from in front of Fredericksburg far to the west, leaving half that number in front of the town to create an impression that the whole Union host was still in place. False campfires were lit and maintained by a skeleton force, as Hooker transferred his main army far up the Rappahannock.

Hooker's men arrived at Rappahannock fords far upriver, crossed over, and got into position around the little village of Chancellorsville, on the edge of the so-called Wilderness, a huge mass of thickets and forest to the west. Hooker was well placed to crush Lee from the rear and the flank. The Confederates would be caught between the troops left in front of Fredericksburg and the six corps stationed around Chancellorsville. But now Hooker was overwhelmed by the same indecisiveness that seemed to attack all those who held command of the Army of the Potomac. He expected Lee to "ingloriously fly," and even if not, to leave his defenses and come out and fight the Union forces "on our own ground." Lee, realizing Hooker's elegant plan, sent the dour Stonewall Jackson on a secret march around

Hooker's position, thus outpincering the pincer movement. Hooker gave up his advantage by pulling his more numerous army back into a tight defensive perimeter.

Dispatches that turned up in the telegraph office at the War Department, where Lincoln waited for the best of news, his feet propped on a desk, indicated that the Confederates were now attacking Hooker from both sides, instead of his attacking them in the same manner. Lincoln felt that a curse had descended on the Union leadership. By May 6, Lincoln discovered, it was all over—Hooker had retreated after high losses, some of his wounded burned alive when shells began forest fires. Lincoln confided in a young journalist, "My God! What will the country say! What will the country say!" The president seemed to have run out of options, and urged Hooker to renew the attack, but only if such an action was not "in desperation or rashness. An early movement would also help to supersede the bad moral effect of the recent one."

At least, a few days after this most "injurious" defeat, Lincoln got good news from U. S. Grant, who had fought so well along the Cumberland and Mississippi. Grant was a man who, unlike McClellan and Hooker, never criticized government policy and considered it his job to make do with the forces at his disposal. He had captured Jackson, Mississippi, and was now engaged in a new attempt, by land and river forces, on Vicksburg. When his assaults on Vicksburg failed, however, he settled in for a businesslike siege. Lincoln did not doubt that, unlike more vocal officers, he would do what he said, and wear Vicksburg down.

After the Battle of Chancellorsville, there were early indications that Lee would move north again. If Washington could be threatened or captured, the powers of Europe would feel justified in stepping in to force a settlement. Lee had seventy-five thousand men to take with him into the North. One big battle, somewhere up there, on the roads that led to Harrisburg or Lancaster or Philadelphia, could save the Confederacy and put an end to Lincoln's war to redeem the Union and free the slaves.

Criticized as a naive military thinker, with an undue regard for the offensive and a lack of awareness of the impact of terrain on the outcome of battles, Lincoln nonetheless offered advice to Joe Hooker that sounds eminently sensible to a layman's ear.

> In case you find Lee coming to the North of the Rappahannock, I would by no means cross to the South of it. If he should leave a rear force at Fredericksburg, tempting you to fall upon it, it would fight in entrenchments, and have you at disadvantage, and so, man for man, worst you at that point, while his main force would in some way be getting an advantage of you Northward. In one word, I would not take any risk of being entangled upon the river, like an ox jumped half over a fence, and liable to be torn by dogs, front and rear, without a fair chance to gall one way or kick the other.

As always Lincoln was anxious to assure his generals that his remarks were mere suggestions, but the imagery of a cow stuck on a fence must surely have lodged in Hooker's fevered mind.

As the Confederates marched north, Lincoln watched Hooker's progress on a vast military map at the War Department, and analyzed telegrams and dispatches with Halleck and Secretary Stanton. Hooker was intimidated by the dangerous possibilities of the Rebel movement, and Lincoln was enthusiastic about the positive ones, the chance the Union had been offered to cut the Rebels adrift. Early in the advance he wrote to Hooker, "If the head of Lee's army is at Martinsburg, and the tail of it on the Plank road between Fredericksburg and Chancellorsville, the animal must be very slim somewhere. Could you not break him?" He wanted a fellow who could see Lee's great movement for what it was, as offering an excellent chance to finish the Rebels off. "I'd always believed," Lincoln would say later, "that the main Rebel army going North of the Potomac, could never return, if well attended to." But not all Lincoln's pithy imagery got a response from Fighting Joe.

The bulletin board outside Willard's Hotel, where Washington's powerful and fashionable had always gathered to read the casualty lists and the latest bulletins, drew great attention. Not since July and August 1861 had the capital been so consumed with invasion anxiety. Hooker fell back until all his corps was stationed west of Washington, but it became apparent from cavalry scouts that Lee had already crossed the Potomac near the former battlefield of Antietam, and was rampaging out of western Maryland into the farmlands of Pennsylvania.

Like McClellan, Hooker gave Lincoln nothing but wild overestimates of the enemy's strength, and demands for reinforcements. Lincoln obviously did not want this attitude in the general. Hooker offered his resignation, thinking it would be refused, and was abashed to find it was not. An officer was sent out to tell Gen. George Meade, "Old Snapping-Turtle," an upright, Christian West Pointer, that he was now to command the army against Lee. Meade, a Pennsylvanian, would "fight well on his own dunghill," said Lincoln. The officer sent from Washington to find Meade managed to do so at 3:00 A.M. on June 28, at a farmhouse in northern Maryland. Shaking the general awake, the courier told him that he brought troublesome news. Meade thought he was under arrest on General Hooker's orders. No, worse, said the officer, you're the new commander.

Meade was a cautious fellow anyhow, and from the time he took command, his chief concern seemed to be, in the spirit of his predecessors, to preserve the army from obliteration. A battle was there to be fought, either along Pipe Creek in northern Maryland or further north in Pennsylvania. The respective attitudes of president and general were a repeat of the relationship between the president and Hooker. As much as the moment exhilarated Abraham Lincoln, it terrified Meade.

By the end of June the vanguard of the Union army was just a little northwest of the pleasant town of Gettysburg. Both armies converged on the place along rustic roads, the Confederates veering south along the Chambersburg Road. Lincoln heard of the opening gambits of July 1. Gen. John Reynolds—who would be shot dead that day—held a perimeter north of the town until midafternoon. His troops were then driven back through the streets to join other Union troops on Cemetery Ridge, south of the town. Some critics have said that Lee should have refused to fight the Union there, should have maneuvered around them and forced them to fight somewhere more favorable to him. But, as he lined his army out along the opposing Seminary Ridge, he knew that everything could be settled there, among the woods and farms along the Emmitsburg Road.

On the second day Lee nearly got around Meade's southern flank on Cemetery Ridge. This end of the Union line was commanded by Mary's old friend-of-séances, Dan Sickles. The Union forces managed by a whisker to anchor their line on two hills, Little Round Top and Round Top.

At the Soldiers' Home in Washington that second day of Gettysburg, Mary came out of the pleasant villa reserved for the Lincolns' use, and boarded her carriage. As it jolted away, the seat on which she sat came unstuck, and she fell heavily from the vehicle. Victorian delicacy prevented an accurate assessment of the first lady's injuries, but her head wound became infected and she became so gravely ill that Lincoln summoned Robert from Harvard to be by her side. No one ever knew for certain whether it was an act of sabotage—the bolts that held the seat may have been deliberately loosened in the hope that the tall Lincoln would fall to the ground and break his skull.

Lincoln himself could not leave the White House or the telegraph office. He received information on the inadequacy of the medical provision for the thousands of wounded, and of the huge artillery barrage that preceded Pickett's charge against the Union center.

By July 4 it was clear that the battle had ended, and the Union had held the ridge. To the relieved Meade, this was the job accomplished. To the joyful Lincoln, the major opportunity now presented itself. He was disappointed when Meade issued an order to his men congratulating them for driving "from our soil every vestige of the presence of the invader." Reading the order, he cried out, "Drive the *invader* from our soil? My God! Is that all?" General Sickles, his leg torn off, had arrived in Washington on a mattress and, fevered and shocked, told Lincoln that Meade had not even wanted to fight the battle, that his generals had had to assure him that Cemetery Ridge was a "good battlefield."

Lincoln now daily expected Meade to pitch in to Lee's shattered army before it could slip south and cross the Potomac.

"You have given the enemy a stunning blow at Gettysburg," he told his general in one message. "Follow it up and give him another before he can reach the Potomac." For some days Lee's army was held up at the river, which was flooded. Lincoln confided to Robert, who was visiting his sick mother, that he wanted to go up there and attend to Lee himself.

By July 14 it was apparent to Lincoln that the Rebel army had crossed south again. Lincoln wrote Meade a summation of his feelings.

> Again, my dear general, I do not believe you appreciate the magnitude of the misfortune involved in Lee's escape. He was within your easy grasp . . . as it is, the war will be prolonged indefinitely. If you could not safely attack Lee last Monday, how can you possibly do so south of the river . . . As you have learned that I was dissatisfied, I have thought it best to kindly tell you why.

Wisely perhaps, he decided against sending Meade this message. As in the previous December, after Antietam, here too Lincoln had seen a way to end the horror and the slaughter of young men, and his generals had not.

There was considerable consolation, however, in the fact that Vicksburg had fallen to Grant. Gideon Welles brought Lincoln the news in his office on July 7. "What can we do for the Secretary of the Navy for this glorious intelligence?" asked Lincoln. "He is always bringing us good news." If ever a man had an excuse for extreme elation and extreme despair, July 1863 provided Lincoln with one. "The Father of Waters again goes unvexed to the sea," the president declared with his usual felicity of phrase. In an unrehearsed but celebratory speech on the White House lawn, Lincoln sketched out a few ideas he would use on a later, holier occasion. "How long ago is it? Eighty-odd years—since on the 4th July for the first time in the history of the world, a nation by its representatives, assembled and declared as a self-evident truth that 'all men are created equal.'"

14

FREDERICK DOUGLASS, the renowned black leader, came to the White House that summer to argue with Lincoln over black soldiers' pay and conditions. They deserved, he said, pay equal to that of white soldiers, and to be promoted to officer rank on merit. And if the Confederacy executed Negro prisoners of war, as was believed to have happened at Fort Wagner, Lincoln would need to have Rebel soldiers executed in retaliation. Ever the gradualist, Lincoln pointed out that there was massive bias in the Union army against employing black troops. "We had to make some concession to prejudice," he explained. Even though he had already drafted an order that Confederates would be killed in retaliation for atrocities against Union troops, particularly captured blacks, he explained to Douglass, "I can't take men out and kill them in cold blood for what was done by others." Apart from Lincoln's sensitivity and gift for realpolitik, Douglass admired him—"The first great man that I talked with in the United States freely."

Amid all this Lincoln had a chance to write to the recuperating Mary at the Soldiers' Home. "Tell dear Tad poor 'Nanny Goat' is lost, and Mrs. Cuthbert and I are in distress about it. The day you left, Nanny was found resting herself and chewing her little cud in the middle of Tad's bed; and now she's gone!"

By the end of September that year, Meade's army and Lee's eyed each other in Virginia. Lincoln was outraged by Meade's gradual approach:

> To avoid misunderstandings, let me say that to attempt to fight the enemy slowly back to his entrenchments at Richmond, and there to capture him, is an idea I've been trying to repudiate for quite a year. . . . My last attempt upon Richmond was to get McClellan, when he was nearer there than the enemy was, to run in ahead of him. Since then I have constantly desired the Army of the Potomac to take Lee's army, and not Richmond. . . . If our army cannot fall upon the enemy and hurt him where he is, it is plain to me it can gain nothing by attempting to follow him over a succession of entrenched lines into a fortified city.

"What can I do with such generals as we have?" Lincoln asked. "Who among them is any better than Meade?"

Not all his correspondence with generals was on the macro business of strategy. Many of Lincoln's letters indicate that no issue was too small for a presidential letter. On October 8, 1863, he wrote to General Meade, "I am appealed to on behalf of August Blittersdorf, at Mitchell's Station, Va. To be shot tomorrow, as a deserter. I am unwilling for any boy under eighteen to be shot; and his father affirms he is yet under sixteen."

There were uncertain battles in Tennessee, and at Chickamauga Creek, General Rosecrans and the Union were defeated. It was essential that Chattanooga now be retained. Lincoln believed that General Rosecrans acted as one "confused and stunned, like a duck hit on the head."

Bad luck with generals was balanced out when the state elections in the fall of 1863 went massively back to the Republicans; and one of the most pleasing defeats of anti-administration figures was that of the Copperhead Clement Vallandigham, who lost the poll for the governorship of Ohio.

That same November, Lincoln was to speak at the dedication of a new National Soldiers' Cemetery on the battlefield at Gettysburg. Lincoln rarely traveled away from Washington to speak, but he accepted this invitation, since it might provide a context for an important message. The ceremonial orator for the occasion was to be Edward Everett, a classical scholar who had been president of Harvard, governor of Massachusetts, U.S. senator, ambassador to the Court of St. James's, and secretary of state.

On the way to Gettysburg, Lincoln traveled with Seward, Blair, his secretaries Hay and Nicolay, and John Usher, his new secretary of the interior. The circumstances were not right for his polishing his short speech on the train. Indeed, the myth would have us believe that his famous Gettysburg Address came spontaneously from a few notes written on envelopes. But a number of witnesses indicate that he already had a draft before he left Washington.

Early the next morning, after chatting with Everett, on whom the chief work of the day would devolve, Lincoln and Seward went for a carriage ride around the battlefield. There were still signs of the battle everywhere, from shallow graves to a redolence of death from the Confederate corpses buried under rocks and drifts of leaves at Devil's Den. Afterward a procession of which the president was part set out from town for

Cemetery Ridge, on which a wooden platform stood. During his two-hour oration, designed to put the ghosts of the slaughtered to rest, Everett pointed out the various geographic aspects of the battle, from Culp's Hill to the Round Tops. This speech was enormously successful, brilliant in the eyes of contemporaries, including Lincoln's secretaries, Hay and Nicolay, who considered it the dominant oratory of the day. John Hay wrote that after Everett's pyrotechnics, "The president, in a fine, free way, with more grace than is his wont, said his half dozen words of consecration."

Lincoln got up at last to deliver, in his notoriously shrill but highly audible voice, and with a skilled, informal, dramatic pacing, his brief dedicatory comment:

> Four score and seven years ago our fathers brought forth on this continent, a new nation, conceived in liberty, and dedicated to the proposition that all men are created equal. Now we are engaged in a great civil war, testing whether that nation, or any nation so conceived and dedicated, can long endure. We are met on a great battle-field of that war. We have come to dedicate a portion of that field . . .

Indeed, he had noticed the coffins at the railroad depot the night before, still awaiting their corpses; and freshly dug but empty graves, similarly waiting, were visible from where he stood. It is now known that the difficulties of identifying the contents of the shallowly dug battlefield graves meant that some Confederates, wearing remnants of captured Union uniforms, were buried among the Union troops, an accident of which Lincoln would probably have approved.

And then came the humble augustness of his second paragraph:

> But, in a larger sense, we cannot dedicate—we cannot consecrate—we cannot hallow this ground. The brave men, living and dead, who struggled here, have consecrated it, far above our poor power to add or detract. The world will little note, nor long remember what we say here, but it cannot forget what they did here. It is for us the living, rather, to be dedicated here to the unfinished work which they who fought here have thus far so nobly advanced.

And thus there must be a dedication to "the great task remaining before us," to take "increased devotion" from the fallen, so "that this nation, under God, shall have a new birth of freedom—and that government of the people, by the people, for the people, shall not perish from the earth."

One historian, Garry Wills, would much later argue that in its exalting of vernacular and biblical oratory over Everett's Greek Revival tour de force, Lincoln's Gettysburg Address made the traditional rhetoric of its day suddenly obsolete: "[A]ll modern political prose descends from the Gettysburg Address."

That evening Lincoln went back to Washington by train, and arrived exhausted at the White House hours later. He felt ill—indeed, he was coming down with a mild form of smallpox. His illness required his beard to be shaved clean. As he recuperated, good news came to the presidential bedroom. Grant had attacked the Rebels near Chattanooga and defeated them at Lookout Mountain and Missionary Ridge. The Confederates had been driven away from Knoxville as well. Eastern Tennessee was safe. "Now if this Army of the Potomac was good for anything," said Lincoln, "if the officers had anything in them— if the Army had any legs, they could move 30,000 men down to Lynchburg and catch Longstreet. Can anybody doubt, if Grant was here in command that he could catch him?"

The Committee for the Conduct of the War had long since asked him to sack the ineffectual Meade, and for a variety of reasons, perhaps even stubbornness, Lincoln had refused. But plans were forming for bringing the effective Grant eastward.

By the time Lincoln made his usual December address to Congress, which he had prepared in his sickbed, the war had advanced to a point where the major issue was coming to be the reconstruction of the Union and of the beaten South. Lincoln called for an increase of immigration, since the United States had such a robust economy, and so many minerals were being discovered in the West. In terms that show that he was indeed a man of his time, he dealt with various recent Indian attacks on settlers in Minnesota and the West, unabashed in hailing treaties for "extinguishing the possessory rights of the Indians to large and valuable tracts of land," and for driving them into reservations on less promising ground.

For the liberated slaves, he held out the prospect of citizenship and voting rights, having by now ceased to emphasize the ultimate project of colonizing the black freedmen. Some members of his own party were uneasy about the idea—if former slaves could vote like citizens, they would end up in Congress.

In a proclamation of amnesty and reconstruction, appended to his message to the Congress that December 8, he disqualified from voting and political office all men who had held Confederate civilian or diplomatic posts, all who had served as Confederate officers from the rank of colonel upward, all those who had resigned from the U.S. armed forces to serve the Confederacy, or left the Congress or the courts to go and ally themselves with the rebellion. The oath he devised for Southerners looking for office was one that declared before Almighty God that "I will, in like manner, abide by and faithfully support all proclamations of the President made during the existing rebellion having reference to slaves."

Mary, still recuperating, in many ways remained a figure of grief. Some of her dead she had not let herself formally mourn—three half-brothers, Sam, David, and Aleck Todd, had been killed in the Confederate army, David at Vicksburg. Now her half-sister, Emilie Todd Helm, had lost her husband, a Confederate general, in the battle at Chickamauga. Emilie sought a pass to come North to attend to business, and Mary, lonely in the executive mansion that autumn, looked forward to seeing her. No one was allowed to enter the Union from the Confederacy, however, unless he or she took an oath of allegiance to the president and Constitution of the United States. Typical of the stubborn Todds, Emilie refused to do so, and Lincoln had her brought up from Fort Monroe to the White House anyhow by military escort. It was a permitted visit so rash as to be politically unjustifiable, apart from the fact that it meant so much to Mary, whom Lincoln could never refuse.

Tad soon found himself arguing with his aunt about who the real president was, the intractable Emilie Helm insisting that it was Jeff Davis. At least one senator, Ira Harris of New York, used the presence of the Rebel woman to argue not only with General Helm's widow but with Mary over Robert's avoidance of the army. The one-legged General Sickles asked Lincoln in outraged tones how he could tolerate a Rebel in the house.

Emilie would have been welcome to stay at the White House indefinitely, since she provided such comfort to Mary. But at last she left to go back to Lexington, Kentucky. From there she sought a license to sell six hundred bales of cotton. Lincoln pointed out that such a license could be provided only if she took the oath of allegiance. When she refused, Lincoln felt he could not in honor budge. With that, Emilie wrote a savage letter blaming the deaths of her husband and other Confederate Todds on the Lincolns. Mary never forgave a sentence that ran, "I also remind you that your minié bullets have made us what we are." Mary felt the accusation so profoundly that she would never speak to her sister again.

By the time the sisters fell out so severely, it was an election year, 1864. Lincoln had grown hungry for reelection, since he wanted proof that his policies had the approval of the people. It had all—the war, the fiscal reforms, the emancipation—grown to be too much for one man to carry. He needed his fellow citizens to confirm that they could carry it with him. But the prospects remained unpromising. Salmon P. Chase himself was looking forward to being nominated by the Republicans, so that Lincoln's very candidacy was not certain. Chase's daughter, Kate, was quite sure that she would make a much better first lady than Mary. A letter was circulating among prominent Republicans accusing the president of being a compromiser, a man concerned with "temporary expediency of policy." Even General Grant was touted by some as a potential candidate. "You think I don't know I am going to be beaten," Lincoln challenged a friend. "But I do, and unless some great change takes place, *badly beaten.*"

Mary, too, harbored secret fears about reelection. The extent of her spending on what her husband called "flub-dubs" for the White House had run up her own personal debts to twenty-seven thousand dollars, and if Lincoln lost, these bills would be sent to him for settlement.

Though many friends advised him to, Lincoln refused to remove Chase from office. It was essential that the party be given its chance to choose between the two men. In March the Republicans in Ohio, Salmon Chase's home ground, would vote in caucus as to which candidate they wanted to see run for the presidency. That would be the great test.

But when March came, the Ohio caucus, outraged by some of the unfair anti-Lincoln letters that had been circulated, chose Lincoln.

He may have been helped, too, by the fact that he had brought Grant to Washington. Meade would retain command of the Army of the Potomac, but under Grant's overarching authority as general in chief. In the White House people greeted Grant as a dour savior. He stood on a chaise, shaking hands with processions of citizens by the hour. Grant had no airs; he spoke quietly and did not fulminate about the fall of Richmond. After such showy but ineffectual generals as McClellan and Hooker, people trusted him, and so did Lincoln.

Yet Grant's plans did not offer a glib or unbloody end to things. His scheme was to harry Lee as he had not been harried before, and try to force him into a climactic battle. The fall of Richmond would be the by-product of that, helped along by the Federal forces at Fort Monroe in Virginia, who would cut the railroads leading from the Southern hinterland into Richmond. In the southwest, General Sherman, with an army of more than one hundred thousand men, would strike into Georgia, seize Atlanta, and cut the South in two. Lincoln was delighted at the concerted nature of the plan. "As we say out west, if a man can't skin, he must hold a leg while somebody else does."

In May, a little over a year after the previous battle on the edge of the Wilderness at Chancellorsville, a frightful engagement occurred in the same area. In indication of his future intentions, Lee had dug his men in there—the war in Virginia was in a way evolving, under the necessity placed on Lee by his smaller reserves of men, from a war of movement to one of fortification. But Grant sent a telegram to the War Department that read, "I propose to fight it out on this line if it takes all summer." Lincoln was delighted to read this dogged cable to a crowd in Washington. From then on, however, Lincoln would have a terrible lesson in the fact that mere aggressiveness, and a gift for the offense, would not necessarily bring success against prepared positions.

Casualties from the battles that brought Grant close to Richmond were more than fifty thousand, and they caused an even greater weariness and outrage in the North. Within the Republican Party, there was a good atmosphere for a challenger, and indeed another candidate for the Republican nomination emerged. At the end of May a group of Gen. John Charles Frémont's supporters came together in Cleveland and nominated him for the candidacy, just in time, for the Republican convention was due to take place in Baltimore on June 7. Lincoln accepted Frémont's emergence with weary amusement. He told, apropos of Frémont, the story of a character back in

Illinois, Jim Jett. "Jim used to say his brother was the damnedest scoundrel that ever lived, but in the infinite mercy of Providence he was also the damnedest fool."

The convention went smoothly, John Nicolay and others watching Lincoln's interests on the floor. A majority of the party still, it now became apparent, supported Lincoln. His chief platform was to enshrine emancipation by amending the Constitution to outlaw slavery everywhere in the land. Thus no future administration would be able to overthrow his chief reform by slave legislation.

The convention chose Andrew Johnson, a Union Democrat and Lincoln's Union governor of reoccupied Tennessee, as the vice presidential candidate. Johnson was a self-taught tailor and former farm boy, edgy about his lack of formal education, rather severe in his attitudes toward the Southern ruling class, but genial toward ordinary farmers, from among whom he had sprung.

15

BUT STILL THE PROSPECTS for Lincoln's reelection were not good. Many leading Northerners had given way to war weariness and began trying to establish negotiations with the South. Wistful desire for an end to the business and a sense of the scale of losses were apparent even in the songs people sang: "When This Cruel War Is Over," "Tenting Tonight on the Old Camp Ground," "Bear This Gently to My Mother," and "Yes, I Would the War Were Over" were some of the songs played by sisters and wives at pianos throughout the North. An earnest supporter like Horace Greeley of the *New-York Tribune,* a devout Lincoln man, initiated his own peace talks with three Confederate delegates on neutral ground in Canada, at Niagara Falls. Greeley spoke of the United States as "our bleeding, bankrupt, almost dying nation." Henry Raymond of the *New York Times,* another loyal Lincoln man, begged Lincoln to open peace negotiations. The South still hoped that it could achieve independence with the retention of slavery, or at least could reenter the Union and retain the slaves. When the latter proposal, reunion with slavery, reached Lincoln's ears, he made clear that it was not acceptable. "There have been men who have proposed to me to return to slavery the black warriors of Port Hudson," Lincoln complained. "I should be damned in time and eternity for so doing."

As summer came on, Grant attempted to outflank Richmond by capturing Petersburg, to the south of the capital. But Lee arrived in time to interpose his army, and prepared for it an elaborate trench system that ultimately ran from the Appomatox River—where it became close neighbor to the trenches shielding Richmond and its railroads—to a point on Hatcher's Run, more than twenty miles to the southwest. This long trench line has been seen by most commentators as a prefiguring of the twentieth century's trench warfare. Lincoln knew that Grant would dig in and hang on ruthlessly; Grant could be depended on to "chew and choke, as much as possible." But the siege of Petersburg was not good for the army—deaths and maimings were daily realities in the long attrition of Petersburg. When Robert returned home that summer, having graduated from Harvard and wanting to join the army, his mother embargoed his enlistment and his father supported her. Eventually he would arrange a place for Robert on Grant's staff.

In late June the president was presented with a chance to remove Chase from the cabinet. He had opposed one of Secretary Chase's Treasury appointments—it was to have been of a Chase partisan—and Chase offered his resignation. Lincoln accepted it. Old Roger Taney, the chief justice who had engineered the Dred Scott decision, having died, Lincoln would ultimately appoint Chase to the Supreme Court. It would prove a wise appointment, since Chase could be depended on to uphold the constitutionality of the administration's reforms.

Arguments over the justice of Chase's virtual firing from the cabinet and over Reconstruction, how the South should be treated postwar, divided Republicans in the House in a season lean in military victories but plentiful in long casualty lists. And as another blow to Lincoln's reelection, a mobile Confederate force led by Jubal Early came up the Shenandoah, captured Harpers Ferry, and crossed the Potomac to attack Washington and Baltimore. Early cut the telegraph lines out of Washington and pushed to within two miles of the Soldiers' Home. Lincoln drove out to Fort Stevens and stood on the parapet watching Union soldiers move across the countryside, driving Early's Confederates out of the fields and orchards. Snipers were firing at the parapet, and a soldier dropped beside the president.

Though Early was driven back, it was one of the issues Lincoln would raise with Grant on a visit to Fort Monroe. How had the fellow been permitted to get so close to the capital? Grant appointed a cavalry general named Phil Sheridan to the Shenandoah Valley to pursue and defeat Early's army, a task to which Sheridan would attend with great flair and thoroughness.

The sinister likelihood was that the Democratic candidate for the presidency would be McClellan—a man who had reasons to dislike Lincoln, opposed emancipation, and was willing to come to terms with Jefferson Davis. But, as the summer came to a close, there were sudden glories: Atlanta fell to Sherman, and Sheridan thrashed Jubal Early in three successive battles in the valley.

It was credible now, as it had not been a few weeks before, that the war was going to end. The fall of Atlanta had undercut McClellan. So did the splendid speeches Lincoln gave to regiments returning from the front on leave after long campaigning. Not altogether ungrudgingly the North prepared to reelect Father Abraham. General Sheridan helped by thrashing Early yet again at Cedar Creek on October 19.

.　　.　　.

On the day of the election, a stillness came to the White House. Few petitioners appeared. Lincoln himself had a quiet day with Hay and the journalist Noah Brooks, chatting in his "shop," the presidential office. He was by no means certain, and dearly wished he could be. At last the sun went down, and at seven that night Lincoln went with his young men, Hay and Noah Brooks, to the War Department to receive the returns. The day had been gloomy, the night dim. No stars glittered with electric hope. The first returns, from Philadelphia and Baltimore, looked good, and Lincoln sent a messenger across to the White House to tell Mary it was justifiable to hope. Later in the night, as good returns from Indiana came in, Lincoln dished out a supper of fried oysters to his friends. By the small hours it had become apparent that he had won. He went to see Mary, then to his own bedroom. Ward Hill Lamon, the Illinois lawyer and old friend whom Lincoln considered a fusspot over security, wrapped himself in a blanket and, well supplied with pistols and Bowie knives—without bothering to tell Lincoln he was doing so—slept outside the presidential door. Lamon was convinced that Lincoln's reelection made him more of a mark than ever, while Lincoln himself was notorious for taking his security lightly.

The next day showed that he had beaten McClellan by half a million popular votes, and won the electoral college by 212 to 21. A massive majority of the soldiers had voted for him—a filial compliment. Yet a number of people commented that after the election, Lincoln seemed even more worn out and aged than before. If one looks at the early 1864 portrait of Lincoln by Mathew Brady, and compares it with the one made by Alexander Gardiner in early 1865, one sees a process of acute aging—on top of the ravages that had already appeared—that is not entirely a matter of light or graininess. Fatigue was chronic with him. Depicted in the South as a bloody Moloch of a man, he seemed in reality to carry the marks of his soldiers' deaths on his angular, inconsolable face. Though there is some argument about who wrote the famous letter to Mrs. Bixby in November 1864—whether it was really Lincoln or his secretary Hay—and though there is even some dispute that Mrs. Bixby lost all five sons in the Union army (she certainly lost enough), the letter is itself a confession of the heinous impact of the war on Union families. "I have been shown in the files of the War Department," runs that letter, which seems to stand for the whole conflict's losses, "a statement of the Adjutant General of Massachusetts, that you are the mother of five sons who have died gloriously on the field of battle." The letter goes on to speak of "so costly a sacrifice upon the altar of Freedom."

Confirmed in the presidency, he prepared his December message to the new Congress. In it he showed some residual desire for colonization—in his praise for progress in Liberia, a republic which "may be expected to derive new vigor from American influence, improved by the rapid disappearance of slavery in the United States." After all, for most of his adult life, he and other antislavery people had seen colonization as the answer to the desired gradual liberation of slaves, without having an impact on the American labor market. The leading abolitionists, by contrast, were offended by colonization, considered that it avoided the issue of whether a slave could become an American citizen, and saw the eventual day when the slaves would be freed as the day they would appropriately enter into full participation in the American polity. Although, as late as autumn

1864, Lincoln sent one-legged General Sickles on an expedition to Colombia, to see if it might prove appropriate for the colonization of former slaves, it had become apparent by now that colonization would be partial and long-term at best.

Lincoln held out the hope that the opening of the ports of Norfolk, Fernandina, and Pensacola would undermine the attractiveness of blockade-running. But the main order of business was the proposed Thirteenth Amendment to the Constitution, abolishing slavery throughout the United States. It had been passed by the Senate, but failed to get the requisite two-thirds in the House of Representatives. He urged the next Congress to pass the measure (as indeed it would).

He had more reason for joy at Christmas than he had had in previous years. General Sherman sent him a Christmas Day telegram: "I beg to present you as a Christmas gift the city of Savannah." Lincoln did not desire further sacrifices of men, but he did hope the war might not end before the Thirteenth Amendment was in place. The continuing bitter struggles and artillery duels in front of Petersburg ended any chance of that.

Now that the Thirteenth Amendment was passed, and the Confederacy so battered, Lincoln let the patriarch of the Blair family of Missouri, Francis, father of his recently dismissed postmaster general, go south to negotiate with Jefferson Davis. Blair brought back a letter from Davis declaring that the Confederacy was interested in any conversation that would lead to peace between the two countries. Lincoln could not swallow the "two countries" idea, but he gave three Confederate peace commissioners passage through the Petersburg lines to meet with him and Seward aboard the *River Queen,* the presidential steamer, anchored near Fort Monroe. Lincoln told the three commissioners that his conditions for peace were that the Rebel army lay down its arms, accept the Emancipation Proclamation, and submit to the authority of the Federal government. He was willing to permit gradual emancipation, to take place in five years' time with "fair indemnity"—that is, fair compensation. It was a remarkable accommodation for him to make, and some would doubt whether he really made it. But on his return to Washington, he called his cabinet into session and told them about this offer. He was willing to pay the slaveholding states four hundred million dollars in government bonds if by April 1 "all resistance to national authority shall be abandoned and cease." The other half of the money would be paid once the Thirteenth Amendment was ratified by the returned, formerly seceded states. The cabinet all opposed the idea, and so Lincoln abandoned it. The terms were unlikely to have been accepted by the Confederate administration anyhow, since the rationale of the Rebellion was to seek to validate the "peculiar institution" as an unassailable right.

Abraham Lincoln prepared for his second inaugural address with characteristic care. As the day approached, many rumors reached Lamon and the detective chief, Pinkerton, that the president would be kidnapped and/or assassinated. "I know I'm in danger," Lincoln confided to Seward, aware that nothing could stop a sniper at the ceremony, "but I'm not going to worry about it." "Assassination," said Seward, "is not an American practice or habit, and one so vicious and desperate cannot be engrafted into our political system." Stanton ordered a company of Pennsylvania troops to camp on the White House lawn, but Lincoln was impatient about the soldiers appointed to protect his person. He specialized in trying to slip away from this protective screen on his evening walks, and there was a story that once he tried to urge his coachman to see if he could outpace a cavalry escort.

The day of the inauguration was March-grim. The platform stood on the east front of the Capitol, and to it came the re-elected president to take his oath, administered by Chief Justice Chase. Here, too, he gave his extremely short inauguration speech, whose opening was deceptively plain and had a sadder-but-wiser quality:

At this second appearing to take the oath of the presidential office, there is less occasion for an extended address than there was at the first. Then a statement, somewhat in detail, of a course to be pursued, seemed fitting and proper. Now, at the expiration of four years, during which public declarations have been constantly called forth on every point and phrase of the great contest which still absorbs the attention, and engrosses the energies of the nation, little that is new could be presented.

Four years before, "all thoughts were anxiously directed to an impending civil war. . . . Both parties deprecated war; but one of them would *make* war rather than let the nation survive; and the other would *accept* war rather than see it perish."

Though emancipation had exalted the war to the level of a moral crusade, the reelected president referred to slavery in only the most dispassionate terms:

One eighth of the whole population were colored slaves, not distributed generally over the Union, but localized in the Southern part of it. These slaves constituted a peculiar and powerful interest. All knew that interest was, somehow, the cause of the war. . . . Neither party expected for the war, the magnitude, or the duration, which it had already attained . . . each looked for an easier triumph, and the result less fundamental and astounding. Both read the same Bible, and pray to the same God; and each invokes His aid against the other. It may seem strange that any men should dare to ask a just God's assistance in wringing their bread from the sweat of other men's faces; but let us judge not that we be not judged.

Everyone, he said, hoped for peace. "Yet, if God wills that it [the war] continue, until all the wealth piled by the bond-man's two hundred and fifty years of unrequited toil shall be sunk, and till every drop of blood drawn with the lash, shall be paid by another drawn with the sword . . . so still it must be said 'the judgments of the Lord are true and righteous altogether.'"

And then came the resonating paragraph that gave the speech its claim to remembrance, and addressed the spirit in which Reconstruction was to be undertaken: "With malice toward none; with charity for all; with firmness in the right, as God gives us to see the right, let us strive to finish the work we are in; to bind up the nation's wounds. . . ."

He did not take time to detail any victories, for he knew they were written in blood in the souls of the people. Nor did he let Vice President Johnson address them, since Johnson, although he was not an alcoholic, had nonetheless drunk too much whiskey as treatment for a bout of typhoid. Walt Whitman saw Lincoln at the White House reception afterward, and said that he looked disconsolate, as if he would rather be anywhere else. Whitman wrote of "a deep latent sadness in the expression."

Lincoln suffered a collapse from overwork and the "hypo" in mid-March, and was plagued by dreams. On March 14, overtaken by chills and exhaustion, he had to invite the cabinet to his bedside for a meeting. But the news from the front encouraged him. When better, he was pleased to go on the *River Queen* down Chesapeake Bay and into the James River to City Point, perhaps ten miles from the front lines at Petersburg. Tad and Mary accompanied him. On their first morning at City Point, Lincoln and Tad in company walked up the bluffs behind the port and looked at the immensity of army warehouses and shipping on either side of the James, toward Richmond to the north, toward Petersburg to the south. This was the logistical immensity his endurance had created.

Robert, now a captain on Grant's staff, arrived to have breakfast with his father, and told him that Lee had tried to break out that morning, at Fort Stedman, just a few miles down the railway line, and had been repulsed. Lincoln set out with Robert on a military train, and saw fallen Confederate and Union soldiers promiscuously entangled in the meadows and scrub, and immense lines of wounded beside the line.

The next day Lincoln was to review Gen. Edward Ord's Army of the James, and to be accompanied on horseback by Mrs. Ord, reputedly a beautiful woman. When Mary arrived during the review, Lincoln and Mrs. Ord rode to greet her, but Mary gave the general's wife a ferocious tongue-lashing in front of all for flirtatiously presuming to ride in the position reserved for the president's wife, and refused to be appeased by Lincoln's pleading, "Mother, please." It was the second time Mary had staged an embarrassing public display of chagrin in front of the army—a year before, the wife of a German officer, the petite Princess Agnes Salm-Salm, had publicly kissed Lincoln in Hooker's camp on the Rappahannock, and this had led to a tiff that went on into the night, and that officers overheard from the Lincolns' tent.

In any case, after the Ord embarrassment Mary retired to the *River Queen,* and she would ultimately return to Washington early.

Toward the end of March, Sherman, victor of Atlanta and prophet of total war, cigar in mouth and cravat tied in a way more typical of a poet than of a general, came up to City Point to see Lincoln and Grant. Sherman's army was in North Carolina now, ready to drive northward. But Grant hoped to destroy Lee while Lincoln was still at City Point.

16

THE CONCLUSIVE MOVEMENT of the Civil War began on the night of March 29, when Grant outflanked the Confederate lines around Petersburg by attacking a village to the west named Five Oaks. Out of a climactic battle on April 1, a war correspondent arrived at the *River Queen* with Confederate battle flags. Lincoln followed the struggle on maps aboard the *River Queen*, but made occasional visits to the trenches as well. On the morning of April 3 came the news that Lee had evacuated Petersburg during the night.

Lincoln took Tad into Petersburg, where they met General Grant, and Lincoln pumped his hand in gratitude. When they returned to the ship at City Point, Lincoln received the message that Richmond too had been abandoned by the enemy. Again Lincoln and Tad and their escort set out, on the gunboat *Malvern*, up the James to the Confederate capital. It was a ruined city that Lincoln, landing on its docks, inherited—the Confederates had fired it. On coming ashore Lincoln was surrounded by black men and women calling his name, shouting God's blessings on him and singing of glory. It was a curious moment. Lincoln, who had bedeviled this city for so many years, was guarded by a mere dozen sailors, and the remaining white citizens, who had not fled to Danville but who abominated him, watched from behind their solemn curtains as a black crowd danced around him in the ravaged and hungry streets. A cavalry escort came and took him to military headquarters—Jefferson Davis's executive mansion, from which Davis had fled. Lincoln walked around the empty rooms and asked for a glass of water. As he sat in Jefferson Davis's chair, he was cheered by the headquarters company.

Lincoln's secretary of state, William Seward, had been injured in a carriage accident and had withdrawn to his house on Lafayette Square. He was appalled, like the rest of the cabinet, when he discovered that Lincoln intended to let the Rebel Virginia legislature reconvene to manage the civil side of Virginia's reconstruction. Seward and the rest of the cabinet began to dissuade Lincoln, telling him they would not countenance the idea of unrepentant Rebel legislators being permitted to continue governing with the consent of the Federal government.

In the meantime Mary returned to City Point, in company with Lizzie Keckley, and the Lincolns visited Richmond again. When the *River Queen* returned to Washington from Richmond late on April 9, Stanton brought the president a telegram from Grant: GENERAL LEE SURRENDERED THE ARMY OF NORTHERN VIRGINIA THIS MORNING.

The next day, the entire city, or nearly so, celebrated. The fine actor John Wilkes Booth, who had been a sour witness to Lincoln's second inauguration, did not share in the national festivity. On the night of April 11 the crowd spilled onto the White House lawn; there were serenades and a demand for a speech by the president. The peace brought "joyous expression which could not be restrained," said Lincoln. But now the question of Reconstruction lay ahead. "Nor is it a small additional embarrassment that we, the loyal people, differ among ourselves as to the mode, manner, and means of reconstruction." He reminded them of the situation in Louisiana, where a Union legislature was opposing the idea of the franchise for blacks. He pondered aloud about the case there on the lawn, and as a result there was merely polite applause when he finished. The puzzled response daunted him. John Wilkes Booth witnessed this evening event as well. Booth came from a Maryland family of actors, and his elder brother, Edwin, was a noted member of the profession. Edwin was said to have saved Robert Lincoln from an accident at a New Jersey train station and was a devout Union man. John Wilkes Booth had chosen to live in the North throughout the war, but hated Lincoln as an American version of Caesar, the destroyer of genuine republican values. Lincoln had most recently seen Booth act in Washington in the tragedy *The Marble Heart*, and did not know how passionately the actor hated him. Booth had set up a cadre of agents, including the Confederate spy John Surratt, whose mother owned a boardinghouse in Georgetown, and they had pursued a plan to kidnap Lincoln on the road from the Soldiers' Home to Washington on the night of March 30, and hold him to ransom for the South's independence. But Lincoln's carriage had failed to appear, and now Booth set his group to kill Secretaries Stanton and Seward. He himself would look to the tyrant.

In the second week of April, Mary, in Lamon's company, mentioned that he looked dreadfully solemn. Lincoln explained that he had a dream which had haunted him. "About ten days ago I retired very late," said Lincoln, according to Lamon:

I had been up waiting for important dispatches from the front. I could not have been long in bed when I fell into a slumber, for I was weary. I soon began to dream. There seemed to be a death-like stillness about me. Then I heard subdued sobs, as if a number of people were weeping. I thought I had left my bed and wandered downstairs. There the silence was broken by the same pitiful sobbing, but the mourners were invisible. I went from room to room; no living person was in sight, but the same mournful sounds of distress met me as I passed along . . . Determined to find the cause of the state of things so mysterious and so shocking, I kept on until I arrived at the East Room, which I entered. There I met with a sickening surprise. Before me was a catafalque, on which rested a corpse wrapped in funeral vestments. Around it were stationed soldiers who were acting as guards. . . . "Who is dead in the White House?" I demanded of one of the soldiers. "The president," was his answer; "he was killed by an assassin!" Then came a loud burst of grief from the crowd.

"That is horrid," Mary said. "I wish you had not told it." But Lincoln reassured her that the dream meant it was someone else who would be attacked, not him, for dreams were never literal.

On April 14, Good Friday, the day of the Savior's crucifixion, there was a cabinet meeting, which General Grant attended. It dealt extensively and heatedly with Reconstruction, but its general mood was exultant. The Lincolns were going to the theater that night, too, since John Ford of Ford's Theatre had sent tickets to Laura Keene's benefit performance of the farce *Our American Cousin*. In the remaining hours of Good Friday, Lincoln issued a number of pardons and reprieves. At about five the Lincolns rolled out of the White House gate on the way to the Navy Yard, and Lincoln told Mary, "We must both be more cheerful in the future; between the war and the loss of our darling Willie, we have been very miserable." There was a note of poignancy in that "must both be more cheerful." He saw, however, his second term ending in peace, and then they might go out to California, and visit the Holy Land.

They were back at the White House between six and seven to eat dinner. Mary tried to beg off going to the theater, which they had arranged to attend with Senator Harris's daughter and her fiancé, Major Rathbone. But Lincoln said that though he was tired himself, he needed a good laugh. Before they set off Lincoln and a detective dashed over to the War Department to see if there had been any news of the expected localized Confederate surrender in North Carolina. Then he and Mary got into the presidential carriage. Mary wore a gray silk dress and a bonnet, and Lincoln his overcoat and white kid gloves. They would collect Miss Harris and Major Rathbone on the way to the theater. At eight-thirty the Lincolns and their guests alighted from the carriage and moved into the theater. The audience gave him a standing ovation. To the strains of "Hail to the Chief," the president and his party made their way to the state box, above the stage.

The play began. The president was absorbed. Onstage the American cousin who had gone back to England and outraged his British relatives was crying, "Don't know the manner of good society, eh? Wal, I guess I know enough to turn you inside out, old gal—you sockdologizing old mantrap." It was at that time that Booth reached the presidential box, ready to kill Lincoln with one shot. He had climbed the staircase from the lobby to the dress circle, sidled past the back row of spectators, among whom the chief reaction was one of annoyance, and flashed a card at the White House footman. The Washington policeman who was supposed to be guarding Lincoln in his box had gone to the front of the dress circle, and Booth being a familiar thespian face, the footman let him go inside to the president. Booth immediately put a single-shot Derringer behind Lincoln's head, by the left ear. The shot entered the left side of Lincoln's skull and exited the right. The assassin then slashed Major Rathbone's arm with a dagger, and climbed down to the stage by the theater curtain, catching a spur in the fabric and falling heavily, cracking his shin. On stage he yelled, *"Sic semper tyrannis!"* and perhaps, "The South shall be free!" Some of the audience wondered if these expletives were part of the play, since Booth was such a well-known actor. Major Rathbone and Miss Harris were both screaming at people to stop Booth, but Booth was not stopped. He escaped to Virginia over the Anacostia Bridge, but would be shot dead two weeks later when the authorities set fire to a tobacco barn near Port Royal in which he was hiding.

An army surgeon came into the box to attend to the president, and tried to clear his throat. The surgeon gave him artificial respiration and massaged the area of his heart. His heart did pick up, but the army surgeon murmured, "His wound is mortal, it is impossible for him to recover." Mary cried, "Oh, my God, and have I given my husband to die?" Fearful that Lincoln would die at once if he was placed upright, the doctor demanded that he be kept horizontal.

Across Tenth Street from the theater was a boardinghouse, and one of the boarders called out that the president could be brought and laid out there. Carried into the boardinghouse, Lincoln lay across a four-poster bed in a back room. Mary, who had followed, cried that she must get Taddie to come—he loved

Taddie so, and Taddie's voice would revive him. The doctors, knowing that it could not be so, led her to a front parlor. Robert arrived, as did John Hay, General Halleck, Secretaries Welles and Stanton, and Senator Sumner. Robert saw that his father's eye was bloated and the eye socket bruised. Sumner held the president's hand as he died. Stanton, weeping, immediately set up a court of inquiry there in the boardinghouse. Mary, visiting the at least moribund if not dead Lincoln, cried, "Love, live but one moment to speak to me once—to speak to our children." The actress Laura Keene, star of *Our American Cousin,* kept her company and tried to console her during the time she was not actually at Lincoln's bedside. He expired at 7:22 A.M. the next morning. For lack of Lincoln, it was Stanton who said the apposite thing: "Now he belongs to the ages."

He had become the bloodied nation incarnate.

SOURCES

THE ABRAHAM LINCOLN PAPERS at the Library of Congress in Washington, D.C., consist of some twenty thousand Lincoln General Correspondence documents, both outgoing and incoming correspondence, speeches, and drafts of proclamations—the Emancipation Proclamation of January 1, 1863, among them—and some printed material. The earliest letters date from 1833 and run through to postmorten documents to 1916, though naturally enough the bulk of the papers comes from the period 1850–65. Series 1 of the papers consists of documents gathered by Lincoln's son, Robert Todd Lincoln. Series 2 are papers gathered by Lincoln's secretary John Nicolay, and Series 3 consists of material from other and more recently gathered sources. I have spent some time in the Library of Congress on other errands, but I live a global distance from it, and reside a four-and-a-half-hour drive from copies of the Library of Congress microfilms held at the National Library of Australia in Canberra. Thus it was a delight to find that the Library of Congress has now been able, through the generosity of benefactors, to place a substantial part of its Lincoln holdings, sixty-one thousand images (some visual items and documents, each page of a document counting as an image), online. It does seem, at least to this lay reader, that they have given us virtually every significant document, and even some ephemera as well.

Many of the documents accessible in microfilmed manuscript at the Library of Congress appear in printed form elsewhere. *The Collected Works of Abraham Lincoln,* edited in 8 volumes by Roy H. Basler (1953), with two subsequent supplementary volumes (1974, 1990), is the ultimate printed source on Lincoln. It is also available in electronic form. It was preceded by an abridged collection, *Abraham Lincoln, His Speeches and Writings,* in 1946, and this is still easily available in a paperback edition. An earlier and famous *Complete Works of Abraham Lincoln,* in 2 volumes, edited by Lincoln's secretaries John Nicolay and John Hay, appeared in 1894.

A printed primary source on the Civil War is the U.S. War Department's *The War of the Rebellion: A Compilation of the Official Records of the Union and Confederate Armies,* in 128 volumes, 1880–1901. Here, among numberless military reports, dispatches, memorandums, and returns of casualties can be found Lincoln's pungent exchanges with generals. Using secondary sources as a guide, the reader can track down Lincoln's graphic style to its place amid the mass of military clichés, evasions, triumphs, and desperations of his commanders.

But a third powerful element in the military equation was the Joint Committee on the Conduct of the War, led by Senators Benjamin Wade and Zachariah Chandler. The Joint Committee disapproved both of Lincoln's conduct of the war and of much of the senior officer corps, which it saw as riddled with secessionist sentiment. Its *Report of the Joint Committee on the Conduct of the War* was issued in three volumes in 1863, followed by another three in 1865. In these volumes we can see the Joint Committee trying frequently to force Lincoln's hand on action to be taken or appointments to be made.

After the campaign biographies of 1860, and those rushed forth soon after his assassination, the first credible biography of Lincoln is that of J. G. Holland, *Life of Abraham Lincoln,* 1866. It is well detailed but hagiographic, and seems in part bent on defending Lincoln against those who accused him of not being "respectable" and of having lacked a settled Christian faith. Lincoln's friend and self-appointed bodyguard, Ward Hill Lamon, published *The Life of Abraham Lincoln* in 1872. This book was actually written not by Lamon but by Chauncey Black, son of President Buchanan's attorney general, and on the basis of materials and oral testimonies acquired by Lamon but gathered by Lincoln's last law partner, William Herndon. Herndon himself had found it not to Springfield's or the Lincoln family's taste when he produced some of this material in the form of lectures. Originally Lamon intended to produce a second volume covering Lincoln's presidency, but the first, raising matters of illegitimacy, marital unease, and theological doubt, became an object of abomination in the United States, not least to Mary Todd and Robert Todd Lincoln, and the second volume never appeared.

At last redoubtable William Herndon himself produced *Lincoln: The True Story of a Great Life,* having to it a credible and gritty texture, in 1889. For me one of the great values of the works of Holland, Lamon, and Herndon was that these were men who had lived in Lincoln's world, particularly in Lincoln's Sangamon County and Springfield. They understood at first hand the politics, the class issues, the tension between antislavery and racism (often in the same soul), and the whole fragile apparatus of backwoods civilization.

Since Herndon's book there has raged an intense and never-ending conflict over the veracity of his sources, many of whom, by 1889, had already followed or were preparing to follow their great friend and acquaintance into the darkness. All the issues of contemporary testimony versus objective evidence or likelihood are brilliantly brought into focus by Douglas I. Wilson's *Honor's Voice: The Transformation of Abraham Lincoln,* 1998, a book that, by testing the legends and oral accounts, gives us the breathing pre-1860 Lincoln. Similarly Wilson's 1997 collection of essays, *Lincoln Before Washington, New Perspectives on the Illinois Years,* deals with issues as diverse as Lincoln's readings in the Library of Congress during his time as a congressman; Lincoln's relationships with Joshua Speed, Mary Todd, and Ann Rutledge; and echoes and dissonances between his political life and thought and Jefferson's.

For many foreign and indeed American readers of my age, their first extended contact with the Lincoln story was by way of Carl Sandburg, whose rich and rhapsodic prose seemed to echo Aaron Copland's music in its evocations of pioneer life and politics. Sandburg's *Abraham Lincoln: The Prairie Years* (2 volumes), 1926, and *Abraham Lincoln: The War Years* (4 volumes), 1940, still make splendid symphonic reading, though they are regarded by professional historians as uncritical in relation to the sources.

My favorite general, modern biography of Lincoln is *With Malice Toward None* by Stephen B. Oates, 1977. It seems to combine scholarship with a lively style and a welcome gift for place and character, and I recommend it as a starting place for general readers. Lincoln's life was so complex that a useful tool to have by one's elbow for keeping track of his legion of acquaintances, friends, relatives, place holders, opponents, and so on is Mark E. Neely's *The Abraham Lincoln Encyclopedia,* 1984.

Allen C. Guelzo's *Abraham Lincoln, Redeemer President,* 1999, is a superb work that, though a biography in a fully adequate sense, places all the incidents of Lincoln's life in their philosophical, cultural, and theological context. Guelzo's work makes of Lincoln's story not merely a record of political and other deeds but a high expression of the conflict of ideas of the time. Guelzo's explanation of Lincoln's uneasy relationship to the old and new schools of Presbyterianism, and Lincoln's spiritual torment over the doctrine of predestination, add greatly to the understanding of Lincoln's soul. The impact of Lincoln's reforms, and their philosophical basis, is similarly examined in James M. McPherson's book of essays, *Abraham Lincoln and the Second American Revolution*, 1991. With a debt to Guelzo and McPherson in particular, I have tried in my brief account to reproduce a sense of Lincoln's governing political principles, since ideas such as those passed on by Henry Clay add a dimension to Lincoln's public and private life that would otherwise go unexplained amid all the incidents.

It is obvious that both Lincoln and Mary Todd Lincoln were complicated and fretful souls. Lincoln seems to have been a sometimes acute depressive, whereas Mary exhibited a bipolar volatility. Perhaps the most famous work on Abraham's psyche is Leon Pierce Clark's *Lincoln, a Psychobiography*. Roy P. Basler considered it too glibly Freudian, tracing, for example, "Lincoln's development of a powerful super-ego . . . to its Freudian source in father-fear."

As for Lincoln's remarkable, all-transforming rhetoric, Garry Wills places the Gettysburg Address in its complex cultural and historic context in *Lincoln at Gettysburg: The Words That Remade America*, 1992.

On the fascinating subject of the Lincoln marriage, apart from Herndon and other sources, we have Katherine Helm's *The True Story of Mary, Wife of Lincoln*, 1928. This account, full of incident and written by Emilie Helm's daughter, is influenced by the quarrel between Mary and her half-sister Emilie. Ruth Painter Randall's *Mary Lincoln: Biography of a Marriage*, 1953, defends Mary's roles in courtship and marriage, and is thus hostile to Herndon and others who depicted Mary as a virago and the marriage as "an ice cave." *Mary Todd Lincoln: A Biography* by Jean A. Baker, 1987, is a skilled modern narrative of Mary Todd's life from childhood to the bitterest end of her widowhood.

For Washington in the mid-eighteenth century, I had recourse to Charles Dickens's ironic if not scathing portrait in *American Notes,* which I read in a 1996 edition of the original 1842 work. *Washington in Lincoln's Time,* by journalist and Lincoln friend Noah Brooks (edited by Herbert Mitgang), 1958, is valuable both as testimony and as a palpable record of place and time. So is L. A. Gobright's *Recollection of Men and Things at Washington During the Third of a Century,* Washington, 1869. Mary S. C. Logan's *Thirty Years in Washington; Or, Life and Scenes in Our National Capital,* 1901, and Mary Clemmer Ames's *Ten Years in Washington,* 1874, are explicit in their praise and condemnation of a capital in which there were plentiful subjects on both counts. The extent to which the South called the shots socially in Washington in the 1840s and 1850s, and thus the extent to which Mary and Abraham would, during his term as a congressman, have been considered outsiders, can be gauged from such memoirs as that of Mary Boykin Miller Chesnut's *A Diary from Dixie,* 1905; from Virginia Clay's *A Belle of the Fifties: Memoirs of Mrs. Clay of Alabama* (edited by Ada Sterling), 1905; and from Sara Agnes Pryor's *Reminiscences of Peace and War,* New York, 1904.

One of Lincoln's secretaries, William O. Stoddard, wrote a series of vivid and engaging sketches of the Lincoln household, Lincoln's visitors, and his work habits in *Inside the White House in War Times: Memoirs and Reports of Lincoln's Secretary* (edited by Michael Burlingame), 2000. To see, from a trance medium's point of view, the scale of the spiritualist shenanigans Lincoln permitted in the White House for the sake of Mary's stability, there is a hair-raising account in Nettie Colburn Maynard's *Was Abraham Lincoln a Spiritualist? Curious Revelations from the Life of a Trance Medium,* 1891.

And so to secondary sources on Lincoln's war. Gabor S. Borritt has published a fascinating collection of essays, *Lincoln's Generals,* 1994, to which he himself contributed the essay "Lincoln, Meade and Gettysburg." Other contributors are Mark E. Neely, Stephen W. Sears, Michael Fellman, and John Y. Simon. Again, here are all Lincoln's most incisive lines on military matters, and here too the prevarications of McClellan and Hooker, the doggedness of Grant, the ruthless, coruscating flourishes of Sherman. Henry Steele Commager's *The Blue and the Gray* (2 volumes), 1973, and James M. McPherson's *The Battle-Cry of Freedom*, New York, 1988, were sources of detail and overview. The latter, however, is more than mere military history—it places the war in its social, cultural, and political context, and seems to this lay writer to be a superbly comprehensive work.

There are innumerable works on individual commanders and battles, a few of which could be named here as having contributed to this work. Clarence E. N. Macartney's *Grant and His Generals*, New York, 1953, gives a picture of the way U. S. Grant fought his remarkable, stubborn war to the end. Stephen W. Sears tells the story of the Peninsula Campaign in *To the Gates of Richmond*, 1992, of Antietam in *Landscape Turned Red*, 1983, and of Chancellorsville in *Chancellorsville*, 1996. Various works originally consulted for an earlier book of mine, *American Scoundrel*, were also useful here. These happened to include Julia Lorrilard Saffort Butterfield's *A Biographical Memorial of General Daniel Butterfield*, 1904; Theodore Ayrault Dodge's *The Campaign of Chancellorsville*, Boston, 1881; *The Second Day at Gettysburg*, edited by Gary W. Gallagher, 1993; and Walter Herbert's *Fighting Joe Hooker*, New York, 1944. Henry Edwin Tremain's *Two Days of War: A Gettysburg Narrative*, 1905, follows the experience of Sickles's III Corps at Gettysburg, and Regis de Trobriand's *Four Years with the Army of the Potomac*, 1889, the memoir of an officer who rose to the rank of general in that corps, certainly contributed to whatever background authenticity the account of Lincoln's war possesses.